VIRGINIA PLACEMENT TEST ENGLISH STUDY GUIDE: 575 READING AND WRITING PRACTICE QUESTIONS FOR THE VPT EXAM

The Virginia Placement Test and VPT are trademarks of the Virginia Community College System. The exams are administered via McCann Associates' College Success testing platform. Neither the Virginia Community College System or McCann Associates are affiliated with or endorse this publication.

Virginia Placement Test English Study Guide: 575 Reading and Writing Practice Questions for the VPT Exam

© COPYRIGHT 2007-2020 Exam Success Group.

All rights reserved. No part of this publication may be reproduced, stored in a retrieval system, or transmitted, in any form or by any means, electronic, mechanical, photocopying, recording, or otherwise, without the prior written permission of the copyright owner.

ISBN: 978-1-949282-65-8

NOTE: The Virginia Placement Test and VPT are trademarks of the Virginia Community College System. The exams are administered via McCann Associates' College Success testing platform. Neither the Virginia Community College System or McCann Associates are affiliated with or endorse this publication.

TABLE OF CONTENTS

Virginia Placement Test Format	1

READING SKILLS SECTION

Reading Practice Set 1 (25 questions)	3
Reading Practice Set 2 (25 questions)	10
Reading Practice Set 3 (25 questions)	16
Reading Practice Set 4 (25 questions)	22
Reading Practice Set 5 (25 questions)	29
Reading Practice Set 6 (25 questions)	35
Extended Reading Practice Set 1 (36 questions)	42
Extended Reading Practice Set 2 (37 questions)	51

ENGLISH LANGUAGE SKILLS SECTION

Grammar Guide

Adverb Placement	60
Commonly-Confused Words	60
Misplaced Modifiers	61
Parallel Structure (Parallelism)	61
Pronoun-Antecedent Agreement	62
Pronoun Usage – Correct Use of *Its* and *It's*	62
Pronoun Usage – Demonstrative Pronouns	63
Pronoun Usage – Relative Pronouns	63
Proper Nouns and Proper Adjectives – Capitalization	64
Punctuation – Using the Apostrophe for Possessive Forms	64
Punctuation – Using Colons and Semicolons	64
Punctuation – Using Commas with Dates and Locations	64
Punctuation – Using Commas for Items in a Series	65
Punctuation and Independent Clauses – Avoiding Run-On Sentences	65
Restrictive and Non-restrictive Modifiers	65
Sentence Fragments	66
Subject-Verb Agreement	66
Subordination	67
Review of Verb Tenses	67

Citation, Referencing, and Plagiarism

Source, Reference, and Citation Guide 68

Citation, Referencing, and Plagiarism Exercises (10 questions) 70

Grammar Exercises

Grammar Review Exercises – Set 1 (15 questions) 72

Grammar Review Exercises – Set 2 (15 questions) 73

Grammar Review Exercises – Set 3 (15 questions) 75

Grammar Review Exercises – Set 4 (20 questions) 77

Grammar Review Exercises – Set 5 (20 questions) 79

Sentence Correction and Revision Exercises

Sentence Correction and Revision Practice Set 1 (20 questions) 82

Sentence Correction and Revision Practice Set 2 (20 questions) 85

Sentence Correction and Revision Practice Set 3 (20 questions) 88

Sentence Correction and Revision Practice Set 4 (30 questions) 91

Sentence Correction and Revision Practice Set 5 (30 questions) 94

Vocabulary Exercises

Vocabulary Exercises (40 questions) 98

ESSAY SKILLS SECTION

Essay Structure 104

Essay FAQs 105

Sample Essays 106

Essay Correction Exercises

Essay Correction Exercise 1 (20 questions) 109

Essay Correction Exercise 2 (21 questions) 113

Essay Correction Exercise 3 (20 questions) 117

Essay Correction Exercise 4 (20 questions) 120

Essay Correction Exercise 5 (16 questions) 124

Answer Key

Reading Practice 128

Citation, Referencing, and Plagiarism 147

Grammar Exercises 148

Sentence Correction and Revision 152

Vocabulary Exercises 161

Essay Correction 164

Virginia Placement Test Format

The Virginia Placement Test evaluates prospective community college students for the skills required for academic study.

The Virginia Placement Test has two subtests:

- Reading, Writing, and Essay Subtest
- Mathematics Subtest

This publication is devoted to reading, writing, and essay skills.

You may wish to see our other publication for the math part of the test:

Virginia Placement Test Math Study Guide: 250 Practice Problems and Solutions for the VPT Math Test by Exam SAM

Reading Skills:

You will see various kinds of texts and the following types of questions on the reading subtest:

- Author's central idea
- Drawing inferences
- Identifying specific details
- Understanding the meaning of words in context
- Assessing the validity of claims made in the text
- Identifying relationships between sentences
- Evaluating the organizational style of a text
- Understanding the author's tone
- Interpreting information in graphic format, such as in charts, tables, or graphs

The reading practice questions in this publication cover all of the skills mentioned above.

English Language Skills:

The exam covers all of the following skills, which are included in the "English Language Skills" section of this study guide:

- Using correct parallelism and modifier placement
- Understanding how to structure compound and complex sentences
- Recognizing correct use of idiomatic language and colloquial phrases

- Identifying appropriate style and tone
- Understanding word choice and meaning
- Using correct forms of verbs, pronouns, adjectives, and pronouns
- Recognizing and correcting errors in sentence fragments and run-on sentences
- Understanding verb tense, subject-verb agreement, and other grammatical skills
- Deploying appropriate stylistic, punctuation, and capitalization skills
- Organizing ideas and evaluating the structure of a piece of writing
- Using references appropriately within a piece of writing

You will see 40 multiple-choice questions on the reading and writing part of the test.

Essay:

You will have to write an essay as part of the Virginia Placement Test.

Essay tips and advice are provided in the "Essay Skills" section of this book.

The essay counts towards 60% of your final score for the English test.

You will complete the essay first, and then proceed to the multiple-choice questions.

Time:

The test will last between two and three hours.

Reading Skills Section

READING PRACTICE SET 1

Read the passages below and answer the questions that follow each one. When you have finished, you may view the answers and explanations at the end of the book.

Equating the whole history of the struggle of humankind to that of the class struggle, the social and political writings of Karl Marx have been the impetus of a great deal of change within society. According to Marxism, the political school of thought based on Marx's doctrines, the working class should strive to defeat capitalism, since capitalistic societies inherently have within them a dynamic that results in the wealthy ruling classes oppressing the masses.

The nation state is seen as an instrument of class rule because it supports private capital and suppresses the common person through economic mechanisms, such as the taxation of wages. Because growth of private capital is stimulated by earning profits and extracting surplus value in the production process, wages have to be kept low.

Since capitalism reduces the purchasing power of workers to consume the goods that they produce, Marx emphasized that capitalism inheres in a central contradiction. Under the tenets of Marxism, capitalism is therefore inherently unstable. Marx asserted that productive power ideally should be in the hands of the general public, which would cause class differences to vanish.

These idealistic writings have had a huge impact on culture and politics; yet, many believe that Marx's work lacked the practical details needed to bring about the changes to the class structure that he envisaged.

1. The primary purpose of the first paragraph is to:
    A. discuss why the writings of Karl Marx have had such enduring social and political importance.
    B. explain the basic tenets of Marxism, before going on to discuss Marxist views on capitalism and the consequences of private capital.
    C. critique the existing class structure and oppression of the masses.
    D. decry the manner in which taxation and earning profits cause wages to be lowered.

2. Which of the following best describes the relationship between the four paragraphs in the passage?
    A. The first two paragraphs state an assertion, while the second two paragraphs refute that assertion with statistical evidence.
    B. The first two paragraphs explain a long-standing problem, and the second two paragraphs provide the potential solution.
    C. The first two paragraphs introduce and expound upon a theory, while the second two paragraphs point out criticisms of the theory.
    D. The first two paragraph give the background to the topic in a general way, and the second two paragraphs provide specific details about the topic.

3. The writer mentions the "huge impact" that these writings have had on culture and politics in the last sentence in order to:
    A. underscore the fact that class differences have not yet vanished.
    B. reiterate the importance of giving power back to the general populace.
    C. lament the social change that Marx himself predicted.
    D. juxtapose this impact to Marx's failure to include pragmatic instructions in his work.

The world's first public railway carried passengers, even though it was primarily designed to transport coal from inland mines to ports on the North Sea. Unveiled on September 27, 1825, the train had thirty-two open wagons and carried over three hundred people.

The locomotive steam engine was powered by what was termed the steam-blast technique. The chimney of the locomotive redirected exhaust steam into the engine via a narrow pipe. In this way, the steam created a draft of air which followed after it, creating more power and speed for the engine.

The train had rimmed wheels which ran atop rails that were specially designed to give the carriages a faster and smoother ride. While the small carriages could hardly be termed *commodious*, the locomotive could accelerate to fifteen miles per hour, a record-breaking speed at that time.

Subsequently, the inventor of the locomotive, George Stephenson, revolutionized his steam engine by adding twenty-four further pipes. Now containing twenty-five tubes instead of one, Stephenson's second "iron horse" was even faster and more powerful than his first creation.

4. The author most probably uses the word "commodious" in order to mean:
   A. small
   B. uncomfortable
   C. spacious
   D. speedy

5. Why was the second locomotive that Stephenson invented an improvement on his first?
   A. because it ran with greater force and speed
   B. because it was more comfortable
   C. because it could carry more passengers
   D. because it contained more pipes and tubes

6. From the information contained in the passage, it seems reasonable to infer which of the following?
   A. Many passengers were frightened about traveling on Stephenson's new locomotive.
   B. George Stephenson's inventions laid the basic foundations for modern day public trains and railways.
   C. Profits in the coal industry increased after the invention of the locomotive.
   D. Stephenson should have been able to invent a locomotive that could run faster.

In December of 1880, a friend who was a veterinary surgeon gave Louis Pasteur two rabid dogs for research purposes. Victims of bites from rabid dogs normally showed no symptoms for three to twelve weeks. By then, however, the patient would be suffering from convulsions and delirium, and it would be too late to administer any remedy.

So-called treatments at that time consisted of burning the bitten area of skin with red-hot pokers or with carbolic acid. Pasteur devoted himself to discovering a more humane and effective method of treatment for the disease. His tests on the rabid dogs confirmed that rabies germs were isolated in the saliva and nervous systems of the animals.

After many weeks of tests and experiments, Pasteur cultivated a vaccine. Derived from a weakened form of the rabies virus itself, the vaccine is administered before the microorganism is encountered and stimulates the immune system to recognize and fight off any future exposure to the organism.

Just after Pasteur had treated his first rabies patients in France successfully, four boys from New Jersey were bitten by a dog that was believed to have been carrying rabies. The boys were sent to Pasteur for treatment. A national campaign was launched, which created a media sensation. It appeared that everyone in the States was following the progress of the four boys, who returned home from France as celebrities. They even went on a media tour.

In spite of the existence of the vaccine, rabies is still responsible for many deaths around the world each year. Incidents of rabies in humans are now very rare in the United States, however. This is because pets are usually vaccinated against the disease. In addition, the vaccine is widely available. However, this was not the case in the past. Many animals and humans suffered greatly from the disease before the vaccine was discovered.

7. In can be inferred from the passage that patients today would most likely respond to the prospect of treatments that were used in the past with:
   A. fear
   B. bewilderment
   C. scorn
   D. apathy

8. The primary purpose of the passage is to discuss:
   A. pasteurization and the rabies vaccine.
   B. the life and work of Louis Pasteur.
   C. Pasteur's discovery of the rabies vaccine.
   D. experimental research on rabid dogs.

9. The passage suggests that the discovery of the rabies vaccine was most significant for which of the following reasons?
   A. It prevented animals from suffering during scientific experiments.
   B. It led to advancements in other areas of medical science.
   C. It contributed to the prevention of the contagions in germs, in general.
   D. It helped many people avoid physical suffering and death.

10. Which of the following situations provides the closest example to the use of a vaccine, as it is described in the passage?
    A. a patient who is given an antibiotic to recover from an infection
    B. a person who gargles every day in the belief that it will help prevent catching a cold
    C. a person who takes medicine after having been told she has high cholesterol
    D. children who get injections to prevent catching mumps and measles

How is civil order maintained within any given population? The civil order control function suggests that public order is best maintained through agencies other than the police force or militia. Accordingly, martial law, the establishment of military rule over a civilian population, is only imposed when other methods of civil control have proven ineffective.

Either the leader of a country's military system or of the country's own government may lay down the edict for the rule of martial law. In the past, this state of affairs most commonly occurred to quell uprisings during periods of colonial occupation or to thwart a coup, defined as an illegal and usually violent seizure of a government by a select group of individuals.

So, how is the declaration of martial law currently regulated? The constitutions of many countries now make provisions for the introduction of martial law, allowing it only in cases of national emergency or in the case of threats to national security from foreign countries. In democratic nations, severe restrictions are imposed on the implementation of martial law, meaning that a formal declaration of military rule over a nation should be rendered virtually impractical.

In spite of these democratic systems being in place, forms of military control are still instituted during times of crisis, with a country's military system being mobilized to support civil authorities, such as municipalities and local police forces. The United States Secretary of State recently commented: "The use of military force to control the population is still a necessary albeit inimical outcome for the governments of certain countries around the globe today."

11. Which of the following statements best explains the differences between how martial law was instituted in the past and how it is instituted at present?
    A. In the past, the militia was not used to support civil authorities, although it is used this way at present.
    B. In the past, countries did not have constitutions or other established means to regulate the declaration of martial law.
    C. There are more threats to national security nowadays than there were in the past.
    D. Civil order was more difficult to maintain in the past than it is during the present time.

12. It can be inferred from the passage that the United States Secretary of State would agree with which of the following statements?
    A. The declaration of martial law is sometimes needed, although it is usually undesirable.
    B. The declaration of martial law is a pragmatic remedial solution when a population is out of control.
    C. The country's military system should provide more support for civil authorities.
    D. The police forces of most municipalities are already over-burdened with other tasks.

13. The last sentence of the first paragraph suggests that which of the following is true of coups?
    A. They usually represent a large proportion of the population.
    B. They no longer occur as countries now have controls in place to prevent them.
    C. They may involve harming government leaders, officials, or citizens.
    D. They have taken place most frequently during periods of colonial occupation.

14. The author finds fault with the civil order control function for its failure to answer which of the following questions?
    A. How is civil order maintained in democratic nations?
    B. How is the declaration of martial law regulated at present?
    C. What constitutional measures exist to regulate the declaration of martial law?
    D. Why do democratic nations sometimes deploy the military to impose order on their populations?

15. It can be inferred that the author of the passage would agree with the basic tenet of the civil order control function for which of the following reasons?
    A. Police forces are well trained and can readily respond during times of crisis.
    B. Public order and civil control are not as important as other social issues.
    C. A country's military can best control the civilian population.
    D. There are occasions when public order can only be reinstated through the establishment of military rule, in spite of the disadvantages in doing so.

A Red, Red Rose by Robert Burns

O my Luve is like a red, red rose
   That's newly sprung in June;
O my Luve is like the melody
   That's sweetly played in tune.

So fair art thou, my **bonnie** lass,
   So deep in luve am I;
And I will luve thee still, my dear,
   Till all the seas gang dry.

Till all the seas gang dry, my dear,
   And the rocks melt with the sun;
I will luve thee still, my dear,
   While the sands o' life shall run.

And fare thee weel, my only luve!
   And fare thee weel awhile!
And I will come again, my luve,
   Though it were ten thousand mile.

16. Which of the following strategies would be most helpful when trying to understand this poem?
    A. To read a little more slowly and thoughtfully than usual
    B. To be provided with more information on the main concepts
    C. To understand the poet's background in more depth
    D. To write down the keywords from each line and memorize them

17. The illustration shows the order of events in the poem:

    He falls in love ➡ He admires his beloved ➡ He declares his love ➡ ?

    Which of the following best completes the illustration above?
    A. They end the relationship.
    B. His beloved leaves him.
    C. He has to leave his beloved.
    D. He goes away forever.

18. Based on its use in the poem, the word *bonnie* most likely means:
    A. absent
    B. darling
    C. precious
    D. pretty

A complex series of interactive patterns govern nearly everything the human body does. We eat to a rhythm and drink, sleep, and even breathe to separate ones. Research shows that the human body clock is affected by three main rhythmic cycles: the rhythm at which the earth revolves on its axis, the monthly revolution of the moon around the earth, and the annual revolution of the earth around the sun.

These cycles create a sense of time that is both physiological as well as mental. Humans feel hungry about every four hours, sleep about eight hours in every twenty-four-hour period, and dream in cycles of approximately ninety minutes each.

These natural rhythms, sometimes called circadian rhythms, are partially controlled by the hypothalamus in the brain. Circadian rhythms help to explain the "lark vs. owl" hypothesis. Larks are those who quite rightly prefer to rise early in the morning and go to bed early, while owls are those who feel at their best at night and stay up too late.

These cycles explain the phenomenon of jet lag, when the individual's body clock is out of step with the actual clock time in his or her new location in the world. In humans, births and deaths also follow predictable cycles, with most births and deaths occurring between midnight and 6:00 am.

Recently, scientists have also discovered that changes in the body, as well as environmental factors, can cause circadian rhythms to be out of sync. For example, mutations or changes in certain genes can affect a person's biological clock. Research also reveals that light from electronic devices at night can confuse our circadian rhythms.

Changes in circadian rhythms can cause sleep disorders and may lead to other long-term health problems. Obesity, diabetes, seasonal affective disorder, and other mental health issues may result from chronic confusion to one's body clock.

19. In the first paragraph, the author suggests that our mental and physiological sense of time is:
    A. appropriate
    B. exaggerated
    C. oversimplified
    D. overgeneralized

20. In the fourth paragraph, the phrase "these cycles" refers to:
    A. the "lark vs. owl" hypothesis
    B. circadian rhythms
    C. the hypothalamus in the brain
    D. the individual's body clock

21. The author's attitude toward owls in the "lark vs. owl" hypothesis can best be described as one of:
    A. disapproval
    B. skepticism
    C. hostility
    D. support

22. The author would most likely recommend that sufferers of jet lag do which of the following?
    A. Better control their circadian rhythms
    B. Take medicine to regulate the hypothalamus
    C. Go to bed earlier than usual
    D. Allow their body clocks to adjust to the time difference naturally

Earthquakes occur when there is motion in the tectonic plates on the surface of the earth. The crust of the earth contains twelve such tectonic plates. Fault lines, the places where these plates meet, build up a great deal of pressure because the plates are always pressing on each other. The two plates will eventually shift or separate because the pressure on them is constantly increasing, and this build-up of energy needs to be released. When the plates shift or separate, we have an occurrence of an earthquake, also known as a seismic event.

The point where the earthquake is at its strongest is called the epicenter. Waves of motion travel out from this epicenter, often causing widespread destruction to an area. With this likelihood for earthquakes to occur, it is essential that earthquake prediction systems are in place. The purpose of earthquake prediction systems is to give advanced warning to the population, thereby saving lives in the process. However, these prediction systems need to be more reliable in order to be of any practical use.

23. What happens immediately after the pressure on the tectonic plates has become too great?
    A. Fault lines are created.
    B. There is a build-up of energy.
    C. There is a seismic event.
    D. Waves of motion travel out from the epicenter.

24. What inference about earthquakes can be drawn from the passage?
    A. There has been no discernible change in the number of earthquakes in recent years.
    B. There has been an increase in the destruction caused by earthquakes in recent years.
    C. The destruction of property could be avoided with improved earthquake prediction systems.
    D. The number of deaths from earthquakes could be lowered if earthquake prediction systems were more reliable.

25. The writer makes her final statement more compelling by preceding it by which of the following?
    A. a dispassionate, scientific explanation
    B. emotionally-evocative examples
    C. a historical account of events
    D. a prediction of a future catastrophe

READING PRACTICE SET 2

In his book *Il Milione*, known in English as *The Travels of Marco Polo*, the intrepid explorer describes the marvels he encountered as he journeyed to China. Upon his visit to the emperor Kublai Khan in Cathay, Polo witnessed the magical illusions performed by the court wizards of the supreme ruler.

Watching in amazement as the wizards recited incantations, Polo first saw a row of golden cups **levitate** over the table as Khan drank from each one without spilling a drop. Polo also recounted that Khan had astonishing powers over wild animals. Unrestrained and ostensibly obedient, lions would appear to lie down in humility in front of the emperor.

However, Khan was venerated for much more than these acts of mere wizardry. Polo's account tells us that the ruler presided over an extremely modern state. Paper currency, integrated with seals of authenticity to prevent counterfeiting, existed during Khan's rule. In addition, his establishment of a vast postal system meant that he would receive news in a fraction of the time that was normally required.

Under the rule of Kahn, the roads of the empire were also well-maintained, and travelers could reach their destinations relatively quickly and efficiently. Although some academics have disputed the veracity of Polo's written account of the Khan Empire, common sense tells us that there would have been little motive for the explorer to have exaggerated his version of events since he was being held captive at the time with no hope of release.

1. It can be inferred from the passage that the primary reason why the court wizards performed magical illusions was to:
   A. venerate the majesty of Kublai Khan.
   B. play a trick on Marco Polo.
   C. provide an interesting story for the book *Il Milione*.
   D. make Kublai Khan and his court appear powerful and mysterious.

2. The author most probably uses the word "levitate" in paragraph 1 to mean:
   A. lift
   B. drag
   C. hover
   D. linger

3. Some academics find fault with *Il Milione* for its failure to answer which of the following questions?
   A. Why does Marco Polo's account go against common sense?
   B. Why should we believe Polo's version of events?
   C. Was Khan's state as modern as Polo described?
   D. How could Kahn have established such an extensive postal system?

4. Which of the following best describes the organization of the passage?
   A. It discusses a problem and then provides a solution.
   B. It recounts a story and then offers an explanation.
   C. It describes a social phenomenon and then illustrates it.
   D. It gives the historical background to a piece of writing and then provides further details about it.

The ancient Egyptians used eye shadow over 5,000 years ago. The cosmetic was used for personal beautification, as well as for practical reasons. Consisting of a paste made from malachite, a copper salt that was bright green, the eye paint protected against glare from the sun, in addition to being an attractive color. On her upper eye lids, Cleopatra wore blue eye shadow made of ground lapis lazuli stone, much like other women of her day.

The queen used green malachite as an accent below her eyes, and kohl, which consisted of lead sulfide, to provide color to her eyelashes and eyebrows. Red ochre, iron-based clay, provided her with lip and cheek color. Henna, a reddish-brown dye that was derived from a bush, was also commonly used by women in those days as a nail polish. The henna was thickened with tannin from the bark or fruit of various trees in order to be suitable for cosmetic use. The use of this particular cosmetic was not limited to women. Men also used the substance to darken their hair and beards.

5. The author would most likely agree with which of the following statements about Cleopatra?
    A. Cleopatra was a typical ancient Egyptian woman in many ways.
    B. Cleopatra was a trendsetter in beauty and fashion.
    C. Cleopatra wore too much make-up for a woman of her social standing.
    D. Cleopatra's use of cosmetics reflected the fashion of the times in which she lived.

6. Which of the following best describes the relationship between the two paragraphs in the passage?
    A. The first paragraph provides one example, while the second paragraph gives further examples.
    B. The first paragraph describes a problem, and the second paragraph explains possible solutions.
    C. The first paragraph mentions a historical event, and the second paragraph interprets the event.
    D. The first paragraph analyzes a phenomenon, and the second paragraph defends the cultural importance of the phenomenon.

7. What word best describes the style of writing in this passage?
    A. argumentative
    B. persuasive
    C. expository
    D. condemning

Dance notation is to choreography what written scores are to music and what written scripts are to drama. The representation of movement in these notation systems varies, although most are based on drawings, stick figures, abbreviations, musical notes, or abstract symbols. Recording the movements of dance through a shortened series of characters or symbols, more than one hundred systems of dance notation have been created over the past few centuries.

In the seventeenth century, Pierre Beauchamp devised a notation system for Baroque dance. Known as Beauchamp-Feuillet notation, his system was used to record dances until the end of the eighteenth century. Later, Vladimir Ivanovich Stepanov, a Russian, was responsible for notating choreographic scores for the famous *Sergevev Ballet Collection*, including works such as *Swan Lake*, *Sleeping Beauty*, and *The Nutcracker*.

Thanks to Stepanov's system, dance companies were enabled to stage these works outside of Russia. Hanya Holm was the first choreographer to copyright the notations of her dance scores, securing the rights for *Kiss Me Kate* in 1948. Two other notation systems, Labanotation and Benesh notation, also known as choreology, are in wide-spread use today.

Apple created the first computerized system to display an animated figure on the screen that illustrated dance moves. Since then, many other software systems have been developed to facilitate computerized dance notation.

8. The passage is primarily concerned with:
    A. describing the history of dance notation and its use.
    B. illustrating the way in which dance notation has improved performance.

C. defending changes to various dance notation systems.
D. criticizing outdated forms of dance notation.

9. The function of the first sentence of the passage (Dance notation is . . . drama.) is to:
   A. provide an example.
   B. set up relevant analogies.
   C. pose a rhetorical question.
   D. state a hyperbole.

10. According to the passage, Beauchamp-Feuillet notation differs from Vladimir Ivanovich Stepanov's notation system in that Stepanov's system:
    A. was used for a different genre of dance during a different time period.
    B. was used for works performed in the Russian language.
    C. was never copyrighted.
    D. was also known as choreology.

11. The passage indicates which of the following about Hanya Holm?
    A. She was a Broadway dancer in her day.
    B. She performed as a dancer in *Kiss Me Kate* in 1948.
    C. She was the first person to register intellectual property rights for a dance notation system.
    D. Her system is still in widespread use today.

12. The author most likely mentions Apple and other computerized dance notation systems in the last sentence of the passage in order to:
    A. advocate the use of computer software for choreographed performances.
    B. identify the systems that have replaced choreology.
    C. imply that computerized dance notation systems are of better quality than those of the past.
    D. indicate possible trends in dance notation.

The Earth's only natural satellite, the Moon lacks its own atmosphere and is only about one-fourth the size of the planet it orbits. The equality of its orbital rate to that of the Earth is the result of gravitational locking, also known as synchronous rotation. Thus, the same hemisphere of the Moon always faces the earth.

The brightest lunar surface areas are formed from meteoric material, while its dark surface regions, called mare basalts or basaltic plains, are the result of volcanic flooding related to impacts from asteroids. Scientific dating of samples from the Moon's crust reveals that the materials range in age from three to four billion years old.

Lunar evolution models suggest that the development of the Moon occurred in five principle stages: (1) increase in mass followed by large-scale melting; (2) separation of the crust with concurrent bombardment by meteors; (3) melting at greater depth; (4) lessening of meteoric bombardment with further melting at depth and the formation of basaltic plains; and (5) the cessation of volcanic activity followed by gradual internal cooling.

Because of the geological and mineral composition of the surface of the Moon, one popular theory hypothesizes that the Moon grew out of debris that was dislodged from the Earth's crust following the impact of a large object with the planet.

13. For which of the following situations does the concept of synchronous rotation, as it is defined in the passage, provide the most likely explanation?
    A. The Moon goes through four phases every twenty-eight days.
    B. A telecommunications satellite is always in the same position above a certain city on Earth.
    C. Two objects fall to the ground at the same speed and land at the same time.
    D. An undiscovered planet has two equal hemispheres.

14. The passage suggests that which one of the following probably occurred after the completion of the process of lunar evolution?
    A. Ice continued to melt on the surface of the Moon.
    B. The likelihood of the collision of the Moon with a meteor was substantially reduced.
    C. Melting at depth still occurred.
    D. The temperature of the internal core of the Moon was lower than it was previously.

15. Which of the following, if true, would tend to disprove the hypothesis that the Moon grew out of debris that was dislodged from the Earth's crust?
    A. An analysis reveals that there are no geological similarities between samples of material from the surface of the Moon and material from the Earth's crust.
    B. The Moon has been found not to have had any previous volcanic activity.
    C. Many meteors bombarded with the Earth during the process of lunar evolution.
    D. A great deal of debris is created when a meteor collides with the Earth.

[1] The discipline of archeology has been developing since wealthy European men began to plunder relics from distant lands in the early nineteenth century. Initially considered an upper-class hobby, archeology in general and archeological field methods in particular have undergone many developments and experienced many challenges in recent years.

[2] Before the field excavation begins, a viable site must first be located. While this process can involve assiduous research, sometimes sheer luck or an archeologist's instinctive hunch also come into play. A logical locality to begin searching is one near sites in which artifacts have been found previously. Failing that, an archeologist must consider, at a minimum, whether the potential site would have been habitable for people in antiquity. Bearing in mind that modern conveniences and facilities like electricity and running water were not available in pre-historic times, the archeologist quickly discerns that sites near rivers and caves could provide the water and shelter indispensable for day-to-day living in such inhospitable conditions.

[3] Once the site has been located, the process of surveying commences. This means that the ground surface of the site is visually scrutinized to determine whether any artifacts are protruding through the soil. The archeologist then digs test pits, small holes that are equidistant to one another, to determine what the boundaries of the larger final pit will be. Once these dimensions are determined, the hole is dug and sectioned off with rope or plastic.

[4] The excavation, which is a meticulous and lengthy process, then begins in full. The archeologist must gauge the texture and color of the soil carefully as the pit becomes deeper and deeper since variations in soil composition can be used to identify climatic and other living conditions. It is imperative that the walls of the excavation are kept uniformly straight as the dig progresses so that **these differences** can be identified.

[5] The soil that is removed from the pit is sifted through a sieve or similar device, consisting of a screen that is suspended across a metal or wooden frame. After the soil is placed in the sieve, the archeologist gently **oscillates** the device. As the mechanism goes back and forth in this way, the soil falls to the ground below, while larger objects are caught in the screen.

[6] Throughout this process, all findings are entered in a written record to ensure that every artifact is cataloged. This activity can certainly be tedious; yet, it is one that is critical in order to account for each and every item properly. Each finding is placed in a plastic bag bearing a catalog number. Subsequent to this, a map of the excavation site is produced, on which the exact in-situ location of every artifact is indicated by level and position.

[7] Finally, the arduous task of interpreting the findings ensues. During the last two centuries, various approaches have been utilized in this respect. Throughout the early 1800's, most fossil recovery took place on the European continent, resulting in an extremely Euro-centric method of examination and dissemination of findings. Unfortunately, as a consequence, the misapprehension that the origins of homo-sapiens were European began to take shape both in the archeological and wider communities.

[8] Recent research suggests that inherent social and cultural biases pervaded the manner in which archeological findings were investigated and explicated during the early nineteenth century because little attention was paid to the roles that wealth, status, and nationality played in the interpretation of the artifacts. These problems began to be surmounted, however, in the 1860's, with the advent of the theories of Charles Darwin on the origin of the human species.

[9] Darwinian theory, the notion that human beings are the ultimate product of a long biological evolutionary process, then infiltrated the discipline of archeology and heavily influenced the manner in which archeological artifacts were recovered and analyzed. By the middle of the 1900's, the imbalance created by the cultural biases began to be rectified as there was a surge in artifacts excavated from African and Asian localities.

16. The words "these differences" in this article refer to:
    A. climatic conditions
    B. soil variations
    C. excavation walls
    D. dig progression

17. According to the article, what do archeologists consider when choosing a potential site for excavation?
    A. whether research can be conducted on the site
    B. whether electricity is presently available
    C. whether the site existed in pre-historic times
    D. whether any data was previously collected from areas near the site

18. The word **oscillates** in this article is closest in meaning to:
    A. inculcates
    B. exculpates
    C. manipulates
    D. vibrates

19. Why are artifacts recorded in a written catalog?
    A. to ensure that no items are lost
    B. to prepare a map of the site
    C. to understand the item's in-situ location
    D. to prepare them for long-term storage in plastic containers

20. Which of the following statements accurately expresses the author's attitude about the Euro-centric method mentioned in paragraph 7?
    A. It was regrettable, but necessary.
    B. It was completely unavoidable.

C. It was regrettable because it created cultural misunderstandings.
D. It only took place within a small geographical area.

21. In paragraph 8, the author discusses biases in order to:
    A. criticize wealthy nineteenth century archeologists.
    B. clarify to effect of archeology on culture.
    C. explain how these problems affected the analysis and interpretation of artifacts.
    D. shed light on the ideas of Charles Darwin.

22. Based on the information contained in paragraph 9, what can be inferred about the early 1900s?
    A. There were few archaeological findings from Africa and Asia.
    B. Darwinian theory had little effect on archeology.
    C. All archeological findings were culturally imbalanced.
    D. Charles Darwin recovered many artifacts.

23. Which of these is the best summary of the article?
    A. An archeologist has many things to consider when selecting a site. Protruding artifacts can create difficulties during the excavation. Most importantly, the European archeological discoveries of the 1800's should be disregarded.
    B. Protruding artifacts can create difficulties during the excavation. Preparing written archeological records can also be tedious. However, cultural prejudices should be avoided when archeological findings are being interpreted.
    C. An archeologist has many things to consider during site selection, excavation, and interpretation. The excavation of an archeological site must be a meticulous and methodical process. Finally, cultural prejudices should be avoided when archeological findings are being interpreted.
    D. The excavation of an archeological site is a meticulous and methodical process. Preparing written archeological records can also be tedious. Most importantly, the European archeological discoveries of the 1800's should be disregarded.

Although there are many different types and sizes of coins in various countries, vending machines around the world operate on the same basic principles. The first check is the slot: coins that are bent or too large will not go in. Once inside the machine, coins fall into a cradle which weighs them. If a coin is too light, it is rejected and returned to the customer.

Coins that pass the weight test are then passed along a runway beside a magnet. Electricity passes through the magnet, causing the coin to slow down in some cases. If the coin begins to slow down, its metallurgic composition has been deemed to be correct.

The coin's slow speed causes it to miss the next obstacle, the deflector. Instead, the coin falls into the "accept" channel and the customer receives the product.

24. Based on the information in the passage, how is the metallurgical composition of a coin determined to be correct?
    A. By its weight
    B. By its increased velocity in the runway
    C. By whether it runs alongside the magnet
    D. By the electricity that has passed through the magnet

25. The last step in testing the coin is:
    A. the slot
    B. determination of metallurgic composition
    C. the accept channel
    D. the deflector

READING PRACTICE SET 3

Acid has been present in rain for millennia, naturally occurring from volcanoes and plankton. However, scientific research shows that the acid content of rain has increased dramatically over the past two hundred years, in spite of humanity's recent attempts to control the problem.

Rain consists of two elements, nitrogen and sulfur. When sulfur is burned, it transforms into sulfur dioxide. Nitrogen also oxides when burned. When released from factories into the atmosphere, both sulfur dioxide and nitrogen oxide react with the water molecules in rain to form sulfuric acid and nitric acid, respectively.

Factories and other enterprises have built high chimneys in an attempt to carry these gases away from urban areas. Nevertheless, the effect of the structures has been to spread the gases more thinly and widely in the atmosphere, thereby exacerbating the problem.

The acid in rain also emanates from automobile exhaust, domestic residences, and power stations. **The latter have been the culprit of the bulk of the acid in rainwater** in recent years. Since the pollutants are carried by the wind, countries can experience acid rain from pollution that was generated in countries thousands of miles away.

1. Which one of the following could be substituted for the phrase "the latter have been the culprit of the bulk of the acid in rainwater" in the second to the last sentence with the least change in meaning?
   A. Automobile exhaust has caused the majority of acid rain [...]
   B. Automobile exhaust, domestic residences, and power stations have equally contributed to the creation of acid rain [...]
   C. Power stations have been more widespread geographically than other causes of acid rain [...]
   D. Power stations have been the largest contributor to the problem [...]

2. Which of the following best describes the organization of the passage?
   A. Scientific explanation and current problems
   B. Chemical analysis and scientific inquiry
   C. Historical background and current problems
   D. Scientific inquiry and possible solutions

3. Which detail from the passage best supports the primary purpose of the passage?
   A. When sulfur is burned, it transforms into sulfur dioxide.
   B. When released from factories into the atmosphere, both sulfur dioxide and nitrogen oxide react with the water molecules in rain to form sulfuric acid and nitric acid, respectively.
   C. Nevertheless, the effect of the structures has been to spread the gases more thinly and widely in the atmosphere, thereby exacerbating the problem.
   D. The acid in rain also emanates from automobile exhaust, domestic residences, and power stations.

Over the past five years, sales of organic products in the United States have increased a staggering 20 percent, with retail sales per year of more than 9 billion dollars. American farmers have realized that organic farming is an incredibly cost-effective method because it can be used to control costs, as well as to appeal to higher-priced markets.

Organic farming has become one of the fastest growing trends in agriculture recently not only for monetary, but also for environmental reasons. Apart from the monetary benefits, organic farming also results in positive ecological outcomes. That is because the use of chemicals and synthetic materials is strictly prohibited.

4. Which sentence or phrase from the passage best expresses its central idea?
   A. Over the past five years, sales of organic products in the United States have increased a staggering 20 percent, with retail sales per year of more than 9 billion dollars.
   B. American farmers have realized that organic farming is an incredibly cost-effective method because it can be used to control costs.
   C. Organic farming has become one of the fastest growing trends in agriculture recently not only for monetary, but also for environmental reasons.
   D. Organic farming also results in positive ecological outcomes.

5. What word best describes the style of writing in this passage?
   A. technical
   B. scientific
   C. explanatory
   D. polemical

Highly concentrated radioactive waste is lethal and can remain so for thousands of years. Accordingly, the disposal of this material remains an issue in most energy-producing countries around the world. In the United States, for example, liquid forms of radioactive waste are usually stored in stainless steel tanks. For extra protection, the tanks are double-walled and surrounded by a concrete covering that is one meter thick. This storage solution is also utilized the United Kingdom, in most cases.

The long-term problem lies in the fact that nuclear waste generates heat as radioactive atoms decay. This excess heat could ultimately result in a radioactive leak. Therefore, the liquid needs to be cooled by pumping cold water into coils inside the tanks. However, the tanks are only a temporary storage solution. The answer to the long-term storage of nuclear waste may be fusing the waste into glass cylinders that are stored deep underground.

6. How are the tanks which are used for storing radioactive waste protected against leaks?
   A. They are encased in concrete.
   B. They only contain waste in liquid form.
   C. They provide a place where radioactive atoms can decay.
   D. They are combined with cold water.

7. Which of the following outlines best describes the organization of the topics addressed in paragraphs I and II?
   A. I. Radioactive Waste in the US and UK; II. Storage Problems
   B. I. Current Storage Solutions for Radioactive Waste; II. Potential Problems and Long-Term Solutions
   C. I. Radioactive Waste: The Long-Term Risks; II. Looking for Potential Solutions
   D. I. The Threat of Radioactive Waste; II. The Creation of Glass Cylinders

8. Which of the following assumptions has most influenced the writer?
   A. The storage of radioactive waste in stainless steel tanks is extremely dangerous.
   B. The United Kingdom normally follows practices that the United States has adopted.
   C. The underground storage of glass cylinders containing radioactive waste is going to be a very risky procedure.
   D. A radioactive leak would have disastrous consequences around the globe.

In Southern Spain and France, Stone Age artists painted stunning drawings on the walls of caves nearly 30,000 years ago. Painting pictures of the animals upon which they relied for food, the artists worked by the faint light of lamps that were made of animal fat and twigs.

In addition to having to work in relative darkness, the artists had to endure great physical discomfort since the inner chambers of the caves were sometimes less than one meter in height. Thus, the artists were required to crouch or squat uncomfortably as they practiced their craft.

Their paints were mixed from natural elements such as yellow ochre, clay, calcium carbonate, and iron oxide. However, many other natural elements and minerals were not used. An analysis of the cave paintings reveals that the colors of the paints used by the artists ranged from light yellow to dark black.

The artists utilized ochre and manganese as engraving tools in order first to etch their outlines on the walls of the caves. Before removing their lamps and leaving their creations to dry, they painted the walls with brushes of animal hair or feathers. Archeologists have also discovered that ladders and scaffolding were used in higher areas of the caves.

9. What was the last step in the process of Stone Age cave drawings?
    A. The paintings were etched.
    B. The paint was applied.
    C. The lamps were removed.
    D. The artwork was left to dry.

10. Which of the following best expresses the attitude of the writer?
    A. It is surprising that the tools of Stone Age artists were similar to those that artists use today.
    B. It is amazing that Stone Age artists were able to paint such beautiful creations in spite of the extreme conditions they faced.
    C. The lack of light in the caves had an effect on the esthetic quality of the paintings.
    D. It is predictable and banal that Stone Age artists would paint pictures of animals.

11. Which of the following least supports the main idea of paragraph 3?
    A. Thus, the artists were required to crouch or squat uncomfortably as they practiced their craft.
    B. Their paints were mixed from natural elements such as yellow ochre, clay, calcium carbonate, and iron oxide.
    C. However, many other natural elements and minerals were not used.
    D. An analysis of the cave paintings reveals that the colors of the paints used by the artists ranged from light yellow to dark black.

Two original forms of theater have emerged from Japanese culture: Noh and Kabuki. Noh, the older form, was originally established to meet the demands of the "discriminating Japanese aristocracy" and remained "unchanged for more than six centuries." Noh renders mundane, everyday activities, like drinking tea or arranging flowers, into exquisite artistic performances.

Consisting of minimal spectacle, bare stage designs, and little spoken dialogue, Noh is classified as more ritual than drama. In order to convey the dialogue, a chorus sings the protagonist's lines while the performer engages in the "solemn act" of the dance.

Kabuki performances are discernably different than those of Noh. Based on puppet theater, Kabuki is designed to meet the tastes of the general populace, rather than those of the aristocracy. According to long-standing theatrical custom, Kabuki performances can be extremely long, lasting up to twelve hours in some cases.

Since movement plays a greater role than dialogue, Kabuki actors must wear heavy makeup and engage in highly stylized actions. Because of its appeal to the general populace, Kabuki theater remains as fascinating and exotic as it has always been, even though its purity has been somewhat compromised through exposure to other cultures.

12. The use of quotations in the passage suggests which of the following about followers of Noh?
    A. They lament the fact that Noh clings on to outdated customs of the past.
    B. They want to emphasize that followers of Noh are traditional, discerning, and serious.
    C. They fear that the popularity of Kabuki theater may diminish the appeal of Noh.
    D. They plan to make Noh more up-to-date in order to increase its following.

13. The last paragraph implies that Japanese audiences today would respond to Kabuki theater with:
    A. admiration
    B. impatience
    C. confusion
    D. boredom

14. Followers of Noh and followers of Kabuki would probably agree with which one of the following statements?
    A. Theatrical productions sometimes last too long.
    B. Japanese theater is unlikely to change in the future.
    C. Theatrical performances should be highly stylized and full of spectacle in order to be effective.
    D. Japanese theater is an important and interesting aspect of Japanese culture.

[1] What's the difference between teaching engineering and economics? Is explicating concepts and facts to others the same procedure, regardless of the discipline? Absolutely not, says Amelia Emerson, who teaches older adults painting and decorating skills. "When I did my education degree at college, I felt it was more for academic teachers than vocational teachers like me," she says. "For me, I felt it wasn't useful."

[2] This and similar complaints are why U.S. educational reformers are looking into a new British project that is underway to assist colleges that train students to teach vocational subjects. The Edge Foundation is a U.K. charity receiving governmental support in order to aid in practical and vocational learning and has agreed to fund the development and approval of new courses. The first 30 teacher trainees are to commence work later this month. Unlike previous teachers in training, these student-teachers, who want to teach vocational subjects like construction and photography, will not have to waste time by composing essays on pedagogy, says Joseph Smith, the college's president. When the students get together, they will be sharing their teaching techniques with each another. For the majority of the time they will actually be teaching, says Smith. "Teacher training should be work-based learning. Students in vocations are not going to learn by sitting in classrooms."

[3] Gary Martin, 37, is one of the new teachers participating in the Edge Foundation's program. After more than a decade working as a carpenter, he is now learning how to teach. "I have taught a few apprentices on site, and I really enjoyed doing it. Nobody's born knowing how to use tools. We all have to learn in a hands-on way," he says.

[4] "Historically, the view of official governing bodies has always been that teachers should have academic degrees," says Martin. However, in the past ten years or so, vocational teaching has come under the spotlight. He explains that "employers of teachers were telling us that while we were enhancing their academic skills, what was really needed was teachers who were better at teaching." Emphasizing that the new courses will focus entirely on subject-specific teaching skills, Martin said: "Trainees were getting a very solid foundation in teaching skills in general, but they were not getting sufficient teaching in their subject areas." To rectify that shortcoming, each trainee on the new course will work with a mentor who teaches in their subject area. They will submit videos of themselves teaching, rather than formal essays, and they will receive special cameras to record their own lessons.

[5] In addition to these reforms, new programs are also underway to improve the educational system itself. The U.K. government has earmarked funds for the Excellence in Education project, which was introduced at various colleges yesterday. The project celebrates achievement in colleges and champions the work taking place under the leadership of gifted professionals.

[6] Yet, across the world, it is a challenge to raise educational standards for everyone. In Chicago, for instance, results for ethnic minority children are rising faster than the average. Thus, what is needed is a far more plural system. So, if a college can attract students and meet basic standards, it should be able to receive governmental funding and students should have the right to find their places.

[7] In addition, U.S. researchers assert that we need a rigorous concentration on academic standards. The government was right to address this problem in educational reforms last year, but we need to go further. We should also reform the exam system to ensure that there is no devaluation of academic standards and college graduates have the skills required for a more competitive job market.

[8] Besides reforming student-teaching programs and improving academic standards, the physical premises where education takes place, namely college and school buildings, need to be considered. An influential pressure group has questioned the value of the government's $45 billion program to replace or refurbish all high schools and colleges over the next 15 years. Governmental officials will suggest that some of the cash might be better directed to making buildings more environmentally sustainable, reducing carbon emissions, or boosting pre-school learning. An increase in university research budgets should also be considered, they suggest.

[9] Again, we may be able to look to the British system for insight. The report on the U.K.'s Building Schools for the Future (BSF) program does not say the program is a waste of money nor recommend that it be stopped, but says the scheme must be regularly reviewed. Many governmental officials also want local authorities to have more freedom over the regeneration of schools and colleges. There have been complaints that the government may force them into becoming private academies as part of BSF.

[10] U.S. Governmental officials have asked whether 45 billion dollars was too much to be spent on the buildings. One official stated: "BSF has begun by providing resources to areas with low levels of educational attainment. Once those areas have their projects in place, it could be argued that investment to replace buildings becomes less of a priority. That might be the point at which BSF and similar programs could be drawn to a close and a different approach to capital and other investment in schools could be adopted."

15. What is the main purpose of paragraphs 1 to 4 of this article?
    A. To describe new educational reforms in general
    B. To summarize the views of teachers to a new education policy
    C. To provide details about a new teacher training program
    D. To point out current controversies in educational reform

16. According to the article, what will new student-teachers not be required to do?
    A. Work-based teaching and learning
    B. Develop new courses and get them approved
    C. Classroom monitoring
    D. Write essays about teaching methods

Fill in the chart below with information from the article: (4 points)

Details of Edge Foundation Program for New Teachers	
17.	Greater emphasis on teaching _____ subjects.
18.	Employers were requesting _____ teachers.
19.	New courses will emphasize teaching, especially in the teacher's _____ .
20.	Each teacher trainee will receive help from a _____ .

21. Why does the author mention minority children from Chicago in paragraph 6?
    A. To demonstrate the difficulty of raising educational standards
    B. To argue for a more diverse educational system
    C. To show that schools need funding more than students
    D. To illustrate the needs of minority children

22. According to the article, what two reforms of the examination system are currently necessary?
    A. Ensuring that new teachers have the necessary skills
    B. Maintaining fairness to minority students
    C. Increasing the plurality and diversity of the system
    D. Making sure exams are not devalued
    E. Protecting and maintaining academic standards
    F. Providing more funding for exams

23. What question surrounds the $45 billion program to reform existing school buildings?
    A. Whether the buildings should be replaced or refurbished
    B. Whether the buildings should be environmentally friendly
    C. What the money should actually be spent on
    D. What the best upgrade of research facilities would be

24. According to the article, what does the report on the Building Schools for the Future (BSF) recommend?
    A. The program should be terminated.
    B. The program should be monitored on a regular basis.
    C. The program should utilize more private companies.
    D. The program should receive more funding.

25. What criticism of the Building Schools for the Future (BSF) program do local authorities have?
    A. They have become less of a priority.
    B. A different approach should be adopted.
    C. They think too much money has been spent.
    D. They may be required to become academies.

READING PRACTICE SET 4

[1] Although improved weather observation practices seem to have reduced the severity of tornadoes in recent years, they continue to be one of the most severe types of weather-related events. While many people live in fear of tornadoes and the path of destruction they wreak, very few people actually understand how these weather events occur. Even fewer people understand how to protect themselves and their property if a tornado were to strike.

[2] Tornadoes develop as the wind changes direction and the wind speed simultaneously increases. This combination of atmospheric changes results in spinning movements in the troposphere, which is the lowest level of the earth's atmosphere. The resulting whirling motion, which sometimes is not even visible to the observer, is compounded when the rotating air column moves to a vertical position. The developing tornado draws in warm air surrounding it at ground level, and its speed begins to increase. As warm air is drawn in, a funnel is produced that extends from the cloud above it to the earth below. The resulting funnels thus become **pendent** from low-pressure areas of storm clouds.

[3] When a tornado touches the ground, a strong upward draft, which is called a vortex, is formed. The vortex is a circular, rolling column of wind that reaches speeds of more than 200 miles per hour. As it moves across the landscape, the tornado creates a path of destruction. These twisters have been known to lift heavy objects, such as large animals or cars, and cast them off several miles away. Houses that are hit by tornadoes appear to explode as the normal air pressure inside the building collides with the low air pressure inside the vortex.

[4] Tornadoes can appear any time of the year, but they are most common during the summer. Further, while they usually occur between 3:00 PM and 9:00 PM, tornadoes can, in theory, happen at any time of the day. Even though these twisting funnels have been witnessed in many places in the world, they are the most common in the United States. On average, there are 1,200 tornadoes annually in this nation, causing 70 deaths and 1,500 injuries.

[5] In spite of having **myriad** sizes and shapes, tornadoes are normally classified as weak, strong, or violent. It is notable that the majority of all tornadoes are categorized as weak. To be classified as a weak tornado, the duration of the event must be less than 10 minutes and the speed must be under 110 miles per hour. Strong tornadoes, which comprise approximately 10 percent of all twisters, may have durations of more than 20 minutes each and speeds of up to 205 miles per hour. Violent tornadoes are the rarest since they occur less than one percent of the time. Although uncommon, violent tornadoes last for more than one hour and result in the greatest loss of life. While a violent tornado can destroy a solidly-constructed, well-built home, weak tornadoes can also cause a great deal of damage.

[6] Because of the destructive, powerful nature of tornadoes, there are many myths and misconceptions about them. For example, some people hold the view that tornadoes cannot occur over oceans, lakes, or rivers. However, waterspouts, tornadoes that develop over bodies of water, can in many cases cause major damage to coastal areas as they move onshore. Additionally, tornadoes can take place concurrently with tropical storms and hurricanes as they move to land. Another myth is that damage to structures such as office complexes and houses can be prevented if their windows are opened before the storm strikes. Founded on the mistaken belief that open windows can equalize the pressure inside the building and prevent damage to it, this action can instead cause severe injury or death.

[7] Because tornadoes have serious consequences for communities and their inhabitants, safety measures are of the utmost importance during severe weather conditions. Drivers sometimes try to outrun tornadoes in their vehicles, but it is very dangerous to do so. Cars and other vehicles offer very little protection when tornadoes hit, so drivers should leave their vehicles and look for safe shelter. Mobile homes and trailers also afford little shelter, so residents of these types of dwellings should go to an underground floor of the nearest building. In the event that a building has no subterranean level, a person should then find the lowest floor of a nearby building and position him- or herself under a heavy object. If no building is located nearby, a person stuck in a tornado can lie prostrate in a nearby ditch or other low area of land and protect his or her head.

1. The best synonym for the word **pendent** in the article is:
   A. churning
   B. increasing
   C. hanging
   D. level

2. Which of the following statements provides the best explanation of this sentence from paragraph 3?
   As it moves across the landscape, the tornado creates a path of destruction.
   A. The tornado causes enormous damage to beautifully landscaped parks and gardens.
   B. The tornado's damage most commonly occurs in municipalities that have been landscaped.
   C. The tornado causes damage to wide-open areas; however, the damage is not normally very severe.
   D. As the tornado travels across the countryside, it creates a long trail of damage.

3. All of the following key facts about tornadoes are mentioned in paragraph 4 except:
   A. the yearly number of deaths in the US from tornadoes
   B. the time of day when tornadoes usually take place
   C. the time of year when tornadoes are most common
   D. the average wind speed of most tornadoes

4. The word **myriad** in the article is closest in meaning to:
   A. limited
   B. extreme
   C. many
   D. average

5. In paragraph 5, what is the author's main purpose?
   A. to explain how tornadoes are classified
   B. to identify the most frequent type of tornadoes
   C. to emphasize the loss of life and damage to property caused by tornadoes
   D. to compare weak tornadoes to strong tornadoes

6. How does the information contained in paragraph 6 connect to the assertions made in paragraph 1?
   A. It shows that tornadoes can move away from coastal areas.
   B. It provides a further example of the misinformation that people have about tornadoes.
   C. It supports the idea that tornadoes are powerful and destructive.
   D. It reveals that tornadoes that accompany tropical storms and hurricanes.

7. According to paragraph 6, what can be inferred about the public's knowledge about tornadoes?
   A. A large number of people know how to avoid tornado damage.
   B. Most people appreciate the risk of death associated with tornadoes.
   C. Some members of the public know how to regulate the pressure inside buildings.
   D. A number of people are not fully aware of certain key information about tornadoes, especially about tornado safety.

8. What is the safest place to be when a tornado strikes?
   A. an abandoned vehicle
   B. mobile homes

C. the basement of a building
D. under a piece of sturdy furniture

9. According to the article, tornadoes are considered to be a severe weather phenomenon because:
    A. many people fear them.
    B. they produce strong vortexes.
    C. they can be placed into three discrete categories.
    D. they can result in death and devastation

10. Select the answer below that represents the two most important ideas contained in the article.
    A. (i) Tornadoes can cause catastrophic loss in terms of life and property.
       (ii) Everyone should be educated about what to do in the event of a tornado.
    B. (i) Most tornadoes occur in the afternoon.
       (ii) Few tornadoes are violent.
    C. (i) Some members of the public are ill-informed about when and where tornadoes can occur.
       (ii) Sheltering in a ditch is a last resort if a tornado should strike.
    D. (i) Most tornadoes occur in the afternoon.
       (ii) Everyone should be educated about what to do in the event of a tornado.

Michelangelo began work on the painting of the ceiling of the Sistine Chapel in the summer of 1508, assisted by six others who helped to mix his paint and plaster. However, as work proceeded, the artist dismissed each of his assistants one by one, claiming that they lacked the competence necessary to do the task at hand.

Described as the lonely genius, the painter himself often felt incompetent to complete the project entrusted to him by Pope Julius II. Having trained as a sculptor, Michelangelo had an extremely low opinion of his own painting skills. Yet, he went on to paint one of the most beautiful works in art history. In spite of his frequent personal misgivings, he persevered to paint the ceiling with his vision of the creation of the universe. _____ . The scenes include the Separation of Light from Darkness, the Drunkenness of Noah, the Ancestors of Christ, and the Salvation of Mankind.

11. Which sentence below, if inserted into the blank in the last paragraph, would be most consistent with the logical flow of the passage?
    A. The nine scenes that he created ran in a straight line along the ceiling.
    B. He was originally commissioned to paint portraits of the twelve apostles.
    C. The Pope also had some misgivings about Michelangelo.
    D. People in the Vatican had grown accustomed to seeing the painter looking tired and disheveled.

12. Why did Michelangelo dismiss his assistants?
    A. Because he decided that he preferred to mix his plaster by himself.
    B. Because their dismissal was requested by the Pope.
    C. Because he believed that they were inept craftsmen.
    D. Because he felt incompetent about his own abilities.

13. Which of the sentences from the passage, repeated below, expresses a claim of the author rather than a fact?
    A. However, as work proceeded, the artist dismissed each of his assistants one by one, claiming that they lacked the competence necessary to do the task at hand.
    B. Described as the lonely genius, the painter himself often felt incompetent to complete the project entrusted to him by Pope Julius II.

C. Having trained as a sculptor, Michelangelo had an extremely low opinion of his own painting skills.
D. Yet, he went on to paint one of the most beautiful works in art history.

Read Passages 1 and 2 below. Then answer the questions. You need to answer based on ideas that are stated, suggested, or implied in the passage.

Passage 1:

Credit card debt is a major cause of over one million bankruptcies each year. The reason is that many people get a credit card without researching and reading the fine print. By the time annual fees are added on, along with spending indiscriminately, payments are missed, which causes balances to skyrocket.

Although we all like to place the blame on the credit cards and the credit card companies, individuals themselves are the real culprits. In short, if your credit card spending is out of control, you need to keep in mind that the real cause of your financial mess is you.

If you can summon enough willpower and strength to manage your finances and spending, then you will find yourself the winner in the game of finance. It may be easy to get into debt, but getting out of debt is much more difficult.

One simple phrase can sum up the solution to financial problems. If you don't have the money to spend, then don't spend it!

Passage 2:

It has to be said that external forces and market conditions have a huge impact on personal financial situations. Have you ever noticed that the things you buy at the store go up a few pennies between shopping trips? Not every week and not by much – just little by little – but they continue to creep up.

But there is a way that the effect of price increases upon personal finances can be minimized: buy in quantity when prices are low. My philosophy is to set out to find the best prices I can get on quantity purchases of such things as bathroom items and dry and canned food, even if I have to use my credit card to get them. You will be surprised by how much you can save, for example, by buying a twenty-pound bag of rice as opposed to a one-pound bag.

14. The writer of Passage 1 would disagree most strongly with which of the following statements from Passage 2?
    A. External forces and market conditions have a huge impact on personal financial situations.
    B. The things you buy at the store go up a few pennies between shopping trips.
    C. But there is a way that the effect of price increases upon personal finances can be minimized: buy in quantity when prices are low.
    D. My philosophy is to set out to find the best prices I can get on quantity purchases of such things as bathroom items and dry and canned food, even if I have to use my credit card to get them.

15. How would the writer of Passage 2 most likely respond to the assertion of the writer of Passage 1 that "the real cause of your financial mess is you"?
    A. You can take control of your spending by making bulk purchases.
    B Market conditions can have a real effect on personal finances. The individual is not always to blame.

C. Sometimes you have to spend in order to save.
D. Credit cards help shoppers to save money in the long run.

Read the passages below and then select the correct answers to the questions. You need to answer based on ideas that are stated, suggested, or implied in the passage.

One of those sprawling flamboyant patterns committing every artistic sin. It is dull enough to confuse the eye in following, pronounced enough to constantly irritate and provoke study, and when you follow the lame uncertain curves for a little distance they suddenly commit suicide—plunge off at outrageous angles, destroy themselves in unheard of contradictions.

The color is repellent, almost revolting; a smoldering unclean yellow, strangely faded by the slow-turning sunlight. It is a dull yet lurid orange in some places, a sickly sulfur tint in others. No wonder the children hated it! I should hate it myself if I had to live in this room long.

These nervous troubles are dreadfully depressing. John does not know how much I really suffer. He knows there is no REASON to suffer, and that satisfies him. Of course it is only nervousness. It does weigh on me so not to do my duty in any way!

I meant to be such a help to John, such a real rest and comfort, and here I am a comparative burden already!

Nobody would believe what an effort it is to do what little I am able,—to dress and entertain, and other things. It is fortunate Mary is so good with the baby. Such a dear baby! And yet I CANNOT be with him, it makes me so nervous.

I suppose John never was nervous in his life. He laughs at me so about this wall-paper!
At first he meant to repaper the room, but afterwards he said that I was letting it get the better of me, and that nothing was worse for a nervous patient than to give way to such fancies.

He said that after the wall-paper was changed it would be the heavy bedstead, and then the barred windows, and then that gate at the head of the stairs, and so on.

"You know the place is doing you good," he said, "and really, dear, I don't care to renovate the house just for a three months' rental."

I wish I could get well faster. But I must not think about that. This paper looks to me as if it KNEW what a vicious influence it had!

16. When the narrator uses the word "it" in paragraph 1, she is referring to:
    A. the room.
    B. the baby.
    C. the wallpaper.
    D. the heavy bedstead.

17. Why does the narrator use capitalization in this sentence?: "He knows there is no REASON to suffer, and that satisfies him. Of course it is only nervousness."
    A. She wants to imply that her husband thinks that she is irrational.
    B. She is trying to point out the gravity of her situation.
    C. She wants to suggest that men are more reasonable than women.
    D. She is praising her husband for being logical

18. This passage implies that the relationship between the narrator and her husband is:
    A. contented.
    B. strained.
    C. resigned.
    D. violent.

19. From this passage, we can infer that the narrator:
    A. is a poor mother.
    B. regrets her marriage.
    C. is suffering from poor mental health.
    D. could be dangerous to society.

20. When the narrator uses the phrase "such fancies" in paragraph 6, she is referring to:
    A. having Mary take care of the baby.
    B. being so nervous about her situation.
    C. her husband's refusal to renovate the entire house for her.
    D. her husband's opinion about her desire to put up new wallpaper.

I cannot say that after this, for five years, any extraordinary thing happened to me, but I lived on in the same course, in the same posture and place.

At last, being eager to view the circumference of my little kingdom, I resolved upon my cruise; and accordingly I victualed my ship for the voyage, putting in two dozen of loaves (cakes I should call them) of barley-bread, an earthen pot full of parched rice (a food I ate a good deal of), a little bottle of rum, half a goat, and powder and shot for killing more, and two large watch-coats, of those which, as I mentioned before, I had saved out of the seamen's chests; these I took, one to lie upon, and the other to cover me in the night.

It was the 6th of November, in the sixth year of my reign - or my captivity, which you please - that I set out on this voyage, and I found it much longer than I expected; having secured my boat, I took my gun and went on shore, climbing up a hill, which seemed to overlook that point where I saw the full extent of it, and resolved to venture. In my viewing the sea from that hill where I stood, I perceived a strong, and indeed a most furious current.

And now I saw how easy it was for the providence of God to make even the most miserable condition of mankind worse. Now I looked back upon my former abode as the most pleasant place in the world and all the happiness my heart could wish for was to be but there again. I stretched out my hands to it, with eager wishes - "O happy desert!" said I, "I shall never see thee more. O miserable creature! whither am going?" Then I reproached myself with my unthankful temper, and that I had repined at my solitary condition; and now what would I give to be on shore there again! Thus, we never see the true state of our condition till it is illustrated to us by its contraries, nor know how to value what we enjoy, but by the want of it.

21. From the descriptions provided in the passage, the reader can understand that the narrator is describing his life:
    A. as a sailor.
    B. on a deserted island.
    C. while being stranded in the desert.
    D. on a cruise ship.

22. What does the narrator mean when he says that he "victualed" the ship for the voyage?
    A. He loaded hunting supplies.
    B. He packed clothing for the voyage.

C. He put on food and edible supplies.
D. He checked that he had bed clothes.

23. What is the narrator's tone when he states: "It was the 6th of November, in the sixth year of my reign"?
    A. sarcastic
    B. mournful
    C. factual
    D. sincere

24. What is the best paraphrase of the following sentence from the last paragraph of the passage: "Then I reproached myself with my unthankful temper, and that I had repined at my solitary condition; and now what would I give to be on shore there again!"
    A. I told myself off for being ungrateful about my previous plight.
    B. I considered the bounty to which I had had access, and I regretted that I had felt lonely.
    C. I beat myself up having been ungrateful about being alone because I longed to return to where I was before.
    D. I scolded myself for not appreciating all that I had had before my voyage and for having felt lonely because now I wished that I could go back there again.

25. What can we infer when the narrator states: "we never see the true state of our condition till it is illustrated to us by its contraries"?
    A. He misses the life he had before embarking on his journey.
    B. He wishes he could be a more grateful person.
    C. He thinks that others could learn a lesson from his experiences.
    D. We learn who we really are when we feel contrary to others.

READING PRACTICE SET 5

[1] According to a recent study by the anti-smoking organization Action on Smoking and Health, movie stars who regularly smoke in films are influencing young people to smoke cigarettes. Psychologists believe they have proof that young film viewers are being affected by the image of movie stars with cigarettes between their fingers. While they accept there are limitations to their study, Sally James and her research team stated that their study found a clear link between use of tobacco by movie stars and higher levels of smoking in the teenagers who admire them.

[2] The questionnaire results, which were published today in the magazine *Tobacco Control*, examined 650 students with ages between 10 and 19 from six different schools. They were asked about their smoking behavior, as well as the name of their favorite movie star. The psychologists then evaluated the smoking patterns in recent films of the most popular film stars. They discovered that 65% of these stars smoked on screen at least once and more than 40% depicted smoking as an essential character trait in one or more films. They found that those teenagers who named a favorite film star who had smoked on screen were more likely to smoke or say they wanted to smoke. In addition, the more their film idol smoked on screen, the greater the risk that the young person would become a smoker.

[3] Indeed, the influence of film stars on teenage smoking now has global significance. According to a new World Health Organization (WHO) survey, three out of four films produced by the prolific worldwide film industry over the past decade show stars smoking. Teenagers who watch film characters smoke are three times as likely to do so themselves. If young people see one of their idols light up on-screen they are 16 times more likely to think positively about smoking, the survey found.

[4] It is the first such study of the vast film industry and part of a new international campaign to cut smoking deaths by targeting the world's film industries. The WHO's World No Tobacco Day focuses on how the fashion and film industries glamorize cigarettes. The WHO survey found that 76% of the most popular films produced worldwide within the last ten years showed some form of tobacco use. In 72% of cases, this was cigarette smoking. "The youth thought it was a very cool thing to do." The implication of that is huge," it stated. "Earlier, only the villains were shown smoking, but now there is a very high percentage of the good guys who also smoke in their films. This research shows a clear relation between on-screen tobacco use by movie stars and higher levels of beginning to smoke by the teenagers who admire them," said the researchers.

[5] They also emphasized that there was no evidence that teenagers who already smoked were more interested in the characters who smoked in the films they watched. Instead the association between star smoking and attitudes that predict the chance of starting smoking was even stronger among those teenagers who had never smoked. "This result suggests that the influence of movie star smoking begins before experimenting with cigarettes. We believe this evidence strongly suggests that media portrayals of tobacco use by popular movie stars contribute to teenage smoking." The results of the study, said the authors, "contribute to a growing body of evidence identifying media exposure to smoking as a major contributing factor in adolescent smoking uptake."

[6] Nevertheless, the film industry is unlikely to react well to the survey. One leading film-maker said tobacco companies, not movie stars, were to blame for teenage smoking.

[7] In addition to the effect that film stars have on adolescents, there may also be other factors that impact upon a teenager's propensity to smoke. Another study suggested that high school children's smoking experiments were strongly influenced by whether they were in a peer group where there were other adolescents who already smoked.

[8] This study, by the Schools Health Education Unit, found that 40% of 12- to 13-year-olds and 60% of 14- to 15-year-olds admitted trying cigarettes last year. This compares to 30% of 12- to 13-year-olds and 57% of 14- to 15-year-olds ten years ago. Smoking among school children has also reached record levels

with three-fifths of 14- and 15-year-olds having tried cigarettes. Of the 300,000 young people questioned, more than half lived in a home where at least one person smoked. Some of the teenagers who were surveyed got their cigarettes from parents or older siblings, while others shared the cost of cigarettes with a friend.

[9] Dr. Edward Adams, research manager at the Schools Health Education Unit, expressed alarm about the increasing numbers of children experimenting with smoking. He said: "This is more than just trying a cigarette. The rise in those experimenting with smoking has been matched by an increase in regular smokers as well. Some of them are starting a habit which may go on for years, and the health consequences are very serious."

[10] Scientists had previously assumed addiction did not begin until youths were smoking at least 10 cigarettes a day. However, research which was led by Joseph Difranza demonstrated that the smoking pupils who showed signs of being hooked only had an average of two cigarettes a week. "Some of these kids were hooked within a few days of starting to smoke," said Dr. Difranza. "Data from human and animal studies leads me to suspect that addiction to nicotine begins, in many cases, with the first cigarette." His team suggested that brains of adolescents, because they were still growing, were more vulnerable to addiction. The effect of tobacco might be stronger and longer-lasting than in adults." Youths can get hooked very quickly and at very low levels of nicotine exposure," Dr. Difranza concluded.

1. What is the main idea of paragraphs 1 to 5 of this article?
   A. The proposed age limits on films that depict smoking
   B. The results of a recent survey by Action on Smoking and Health
   C. The impact of the film industry's portrayal of smoking on adolescent tobacco use
   D. The process of nicotine addiction in teenagers

2. What percentage of films produced worldwide in the last ten years depicted tobacco use?
   A. 65%
   B. 40%
   C. 76%
   D. 72%

3. Which best summarizes the Focus of WHO's No Tobacco Day?
   A. To reveal that tobacco-related illness is geographically disproportionate
   B. To address how tobacco use is portrayed in industries that affect young people
   C. To bring about limitations on cigarette advertising
   D. To publicize the number of tobacco-related deaths

4. According to the WHO, what was the most significant finding about tobacco use at the time the article was written?
   A. Portrayals of tobacco use in movies are more frequent.
   B. The influence of movie star smoking begins before experimenting with cigarettes.
   C. The chance of starting smoking was even stronger among those teenagers who had never smoked.
   D. There is a clear relationship between smoking in media and film and increased levels of teenage smoking.

5. According to the article, what three factors most affect an adolescent's desire to smoke?
   A. Influence by the tobacco industry
   B. Whether their friends smoke
   C. If they see smoking as something "cool"
   D. Schools Health Education Unit
   E. Whether someone in their home already smokes
   F. The frequency of WHO No Tobacco Day
   G. The cost of cigarettes

6. What is the purpose of paragraph 6 of the article?
   A. To reveal that tobacco companies cannot be relied upon
   B. To show how the film and tobacco industries clash with one another
   C. To show how easy it is to shift the blame for adolescent tobacco use
   D. To identify contributing factors to teen smoking

7. How does the information provided in paragraph 8 contribute to the development of ideas in the article?
   A. It provides important statistics that quantify his claims about teenage smoking.
   B. It offers a useful anecdote that casts light on teenage smoking.
   C. It illustrates that teenage smoking live in households with other smokers.
   D. It supports the theories that scientists previously had about addiction.

8. According to Dr. Edward Adams, which one of the following statements is correct?
   A. The increase in experimental smoking is less than that of regular smoking
   B. The increase in experimental smoking is accompanied by an increase in that of regular smoking
   C. The increase in experimental smoking is more than that of regular smoking
   D. The increase in experimental smoking is accompanied by a decrease in that of regular smoking

9. When considering the results of various recent studies, what has caused the most alarm among researchers?
   A. The overall rise in teen smoking compared to past adolescent tobacco use.
   B. The fact that teenagers are getting addicted more easily and quickly than before.
   C. The fact that most teen smokers have at least 10 cigarettes a day.
   D. The fact that girls become addicted to smoking much more quickly than boys.

10. Why are teenagers more susceptible to nicotine addiction?
    A. Because of peer pressure from their friends
    B. Because of insufficient monitoring at school and at home
    C. Because their brains are not fully developed
    D. Because they had an average of two cigarettes a week

Today archeologists are still endeavoring to uncover the secrets of Africa's past. Evidence of the earliest human activity has been found in the south and east of the continent, where climatic conditions helped to preserve the human skeletons and stone tools found there.

Genetic science confirms that these are quite likely the oldest remains in the world of modern people, with this classification based on the ability of humans to become adaptable and ready to respond to environmental change. Even though the artifacts and skeletons of early Africans are most commonly found in a highly fragmented state, these findings are more than sufficient in order to make a number of significant conclusions.

Perhaps the most important discovery is that there is great **variation** among the human remains, indicating a wide array of physical differences among members of the population. While the early population was diverse, it has been well established that the earliest species of hominids spread from Africa to other continents.

The first traces of human technology, consisting of simple stone tools, were also discovered in Africa. Having been developed long before the invention of metallurgy, tools had gradually become smaller and more sophisticated. Microliths, fine stone tools that were fitted to handles, were used as cutting and scraping tools and may even have been the precursor to the bow and arrow.

11. Which of the following best describes the organization of the passage?
    A. A common fallacy is described, and then it is refuted.
    B. An unresolved question is posed, and then it is answered.
    C. A problem is described, and then a solution is discussed.
    D. General information about the research is provided, and then the specific findings of the research are presented.

12. The author states that "genetic science confirms that these are quite likely the oldest remains in the world of modern people" in paragraph 2 primarily in order to emphasize:
    A. the depth and breadth of Africa's history.
    B. the way that climatic conditions can help to preserve skeletons.
    C. the importance of the stone tools found in African sites.
    D. the significance of archeological discoveries in Africa.

13. As used in paragraph 3, the word "variation" most likely means:
    A. distinction
    B. discrepancy
    C. possibility for error
    D. variety

14. From the passage, it can be inferred that some of the archeological discoveries from Africa:
    A. were broken into small pieces or extremely damaged.
    B. would not have been located without modern genetic science.
    C. were not as important as those from other continents.
    D. supported the development of metallurgy.

15. The passage suggests that the discovery of microliths was significant for which one of the following reasons?
    A. Microliths illustrate the importance of the invention of the bow and arrow.
    B. Microliths demonstrate the level of sophistication and ingenuity of the prehistoric African population.
    C. Microliths support the view that hominids spread to other continents.
    D. Microliths show that technology at that time consisted of more than stone tools.

Read the passages and then select the correct answers to the questions. You need to answer based on ideas that are stated, suggested, or implied in the passage.

The excellent Mr. Morris was an Englishman, and he lived in the days of Queen Victoria the Good. He was a prosperous and very sensible man; he read the Times and went to church, and as he grew towards middle age an expression of quiet contented contempt for all who were not as himself settled. Everything that it was right and proper for a man in his position to possess, he possessed.

And among other right and proper possessions, this Mr. Morris had a wife and children. They were the right sort of wife, and the right sort and number of children, of course; nothing imaginative or highty-flighty about any of them, so far as Mr. Morris could see; they wore perfectly correct clothing, neither smart nor hygienic nor faddy in any way; and they lived in a nice sensible house.

And when it was a fit and proper thing for him to do so, Mr. Morris died. His tomb was of marble, and, without any art nonsense or laudatory inscription, quietly imposing—such being the fashion of his time.

He underwent various changes according to the accepted custom in these cases, and long before this story begins his bones even had become dust, and were scattered to the four quarters of heaven. And his sons and his grandsons and his great-grandsons and his great-great-grandsons, they too were dust and ashes, and were scattered likewise. It was a thing he could not have imagined, that a day would come when even his great-great-grandsons would be scattered to the four winds of heaven. If anyone had suggested it to him he would have resented it.

He was one of those worthy people who take no interest in the future of mankind at all. He had grave doubts, indeed, if there was any future for mankind after he was dead. It seemed quite impossible and quite uninteresting to imagine anything happening after he was dead. Yet the thing was so, and when even his great-great-grandson was dead and decayed and forgotten, when the sham half-timbered house had gone the way of all shams, and all that Mr. Morris had found real and important was sere and dead, the world was still going on, and people were still going about it, just as heedless and impatient of the Future, or, indeed, of anything but their own selves and property, as Mr. Morris had been.

16. What does the narrator imply when he states "And among other right and proper possessions, this Mr. Morris had a wife and children"?
    A. Mr. Morris felt affection toward his wife and children, although he sometimes treated them coldly.
    B. Mr. Morris got married and had a family because social convention dictated that he do so.
    C. Mr. Morris quietly resented his wife and family because they made him acquire possessions that he did not want.
    D. Mr. Morris's family awaited his passing because it meant they would come into a good inheritance.

17. What is the best meaning of "highty-flighty" as it is used in paragraph 2?
    A. frivolous
    B. erudite
    C. sensitive
    D. unfriendly

18. What is the best paraphrase of this phrase: "when the sham half-timbered house had gone the way of all shams?"
    A. when Mr. Morris was long dead and his possessions were gone and forgotten
    B. when Mr. Morris's great-grandsons had forgotten about the house and their great-grandfather
    C. when the precious home had decayed and was scattered like ash and dust
    D. when the pretentious dwelling was gone and forgotten, like all worldly possessions

19. The description of Mr. Morris's home and his tomb are similar because:
    A. they demonstrated no real interest in the future of mankind.
    B. they displayed the underlying resentment that Mr. Morris felt about his life.
    C. they would have been considered right and proper for the society of their time.
    D. they both reveal the heed and care that society takes about the future.

20. From the tone of this passage, the reader could assume that the story is going to be about:
    A. how life in the future is different than life in the past.
    B. the narrator's regrets with his grandchildren.
    C. the protagonist's home and other possessions.
    D. spiritual aspects of the afterlife.

Oliver, having taken down the shutters, was graciously assisted by Noah, who having consoled him with the assurance that "he'd catch it," condescended to help him. Mr. Snowberry came down soon after.

Shortly afterwards, Mrs. Snowberry appeared. Oliver having "caught it," in fulfillment of Noah's prediction, followed the young gentleman down the stairs to breakfast.

"Come near the fire, Noah," said Charlotte. "I have saved a nice little bit of bacon for you from master's breakfast."

"Do you hear?" said Noah.

"Lord, Noah!" said Charlotte.

"Let him alone!" said Noah. "Why everybody lets him alone enough, for the matter of that."

"Oh, you queer soul!" said Charlotte, bursting into a hearty laugh. She was then joined by Noah, after which they both looked scornfully at poor Oliver Twist.

Noah was a charity boy, but not a workhouse orphan. He could trace his genealogy back to his parents, who lived hard by; his mother being a washerwoman, and his father a drunken soldier, discharged with a wooden leg, and a diurnal pension of twopence-halfpenny and an unstable fraction. The shop boys in the neighborhood had long been in the habit of branding Noah, in the public streets, with the ignominious epithets of "leathers," "charity," and the like; and Noah had borne them without reply. But now that fortune had cast his way a nameless orphan, at whom even the meanest could point the finger of scorn, he retorted on him with interest.

21. What is the meaning of "he'd catch it" in the first paragraph of the passage?
    A. he'd find it
    B. he'd be saved
    C. he would be laughed at
    D. he would be punished

22. From paragraph 3, the reader can surmise that Charlotte is:
    A. the Snowberry's daughter.
    B. Noah's sister.
    C. Oliver's sister.
    D. an employee of the Snowberry family.

23. According to the passage, Oliver could be described as:
    A. gracious.
    B. scornful.
    C. ignominious.
    D. ridiculed.

24. The passage mainly illustrates:
    A. Charlotte's contempt of orphans.
    B. the wealth of the Snowberry family.
    C. the adventures and exploits of Oliver.
    D. the relationship between Noah and Oliver.

25. Who is the "nameless orphan" mentioned in the passage?
    A. charity boys
    B. workhouse orphans
    C. Noah
    D. Oliver

READING PRACTICE SET 6

[1] Scientists have been able to clone mice for the very first time by using stem cells harvested from the hairs of mature animals. The procedure is much more efficient than cloning with the use of adult cells, and it could be used to create individualized therapies for those suffering from Alzheimer's and Parkinson's diseases. In the past, mice had been cloned with the use of adult cells, but it was a very inefficient process.

[2] In the long term, scientists want to use such legalized cloning to generate therapies. A patient's skin cell could generate a cloned embryo which is grown for just a few days, at which point it is the size of a pin head. If embryonic stem cells, which can turn into any type of tissue, were harvested from the early-stage embryo they could be used to regenerate damaged tissue which is genetically matched to a patient. This would avoid immune rejection.

[3] The public's response to this embryonic stem cell cloning technique is mixed. Yet perhaps surprisingly, 59% of those surveyed agreed with controversial research, according to figures released by the International Council on Medicine (ICM). The slight majority of respondents, 51% supported genetic engineering when used to correct physical defects in the fetus. This demonstrates that public attitudes toward genetic engineering have undergone a positive change, and it also bodes well for scientists who assert that cloning is the best way to find cures for some of society's most serious genetic disorders.

[4] Although the majority of the public condones the use of genetic engineering to cure illness or assist with organ transplants, many still resist the idea of parents creating "designer babies." The ICM survey results revealed that only 13% of respondents were in support of the parents using genetic engineering to "design" an unborn child, with 63% opposing such use. A marginally higher result, 20% of 18- to 24-year-olds said they would support the practice, which implies that future generations may be more open-minded about the idea.

[5] Currently, it is only legally possible to carry out two kinds of reproductive assistance on humans using In Vitro Fertilization to fertilize eggs outside the mother's body. The first procedure involves determining the genes and sex of the unborn baby. The second technique, called Pre-implantation Genetic Diagnosis, conducts embryo screening for genetic diseases, with only selected embryos implanted into the mother's womb. In the future, we may be able to use what is called germ line therapy to "cure" genetic diseases in embryos by substituting healthy DNA for faulty sections of DNA. Such therapy has been carried out on animal embryos successfully, but it is currently illegal to do this procedure on human embryos.

[6] Fears are that cloning techniques will be taken even further and used to screen personality traits in the unborn child, from their hair or eye color to their ability to perform well in sports or exams. While it may be years before public opinion truly supports us "designing" unborn children, scientists have the public's go-ahead to continue utilizing genetic engineering to help us all live healthier, longer lives.

[7] The advancement of genetic engineering has also been supported by the recent human genome project. Scientists and their publicists have used words and phrases such as "renaissance," "holy grail," and "the book of life" to describe this project, which they see as having huge benefits for health care worldwide. Nevertheless, like the new cloning technique described above, the human genome project also has its critics. Its detractors insist that its defining feature is simply its larger size. Furthermore, they claim that its supporters' worship of size is a fitting signifier for science in an era of globalization and multinational corporations. However, it is a better understanding of organisms, and therefore of disease, which many people see as the true promise of the human genome.

[8] We are promised genetic tests that will tell us whether we are susceptible to heart disease or cancer. Yet, what will we do with this information? And do we even want it? There is evidence that most people who may be at risk from Huntington's disease, which kills in middle age and for which there is no cure, do not want to know if they have the gene. Even if we can change our lifestyles, will we do so? Many people

may treat susceptibility-prediction as inevitability and relapse into even worse lifestyles. Only one thing seems certain: the designing of new treatments targeted at genes involved in disease will be massively complicated because of the involvement of many different genes.

1. What is the main idea of this article?
   A. To describe new developments in the cloning of mice
   B. To summarize the public's views on genetic engineering
   C. To support the human genome project
   D. To discuss new developments in genetic engineering and their related debates

2. What is the disadvantage of the use of the adult cells of mice for cloning?
   A. It cannot be used for certain diseases.
   B. It cannot be used with all types of tissue.
   C. It can be less efficient than other cloning methods.
   D. Its effectiveness has not been proven.

3. What are the benefits of generating early-stage embryos?
   A. They can be used as tissue transplants.
   B. They will help in the process of legalizing cloning.
   C. They are very compact in size.
   D. They will help reduce tissue rejection.

4. At present, what two reproductive methods have been legalized for humans?
   A. Germ line therapy
   B. Sex and gene determination
   C. Embryo screening
   D. Advanced reproductive technologies
   E. Genetic characteristic selection
   F. Genetically-designed children

5. Which of the following is a criticism of the human genome project?
   A. It is not available worldwide.
   B. Its only unique aspect is its size.
   C. It will only help multinational corporations.
   D. It will be impeded by advancing globalization.

6. What potential negative outcome could occur when a person receives the results of a genetic test?
   A. People with incurable illnesses may stop taking care of themselves.
   B. They may not be able to get the drugs they need.
   C. They may not allow their information to be used for research purposes.
   D. People will not be allowed to take the test voluntarily.

The pyramids at Giza in Egypt are still among the world's largest structures, even today. The monuments were constructed well before the wheel was invented, and it is notable that the Egyptians had only the most primitive, handmade tools to complete the massive project.

Copper saws were used to cut softer stones, as well as the large wooden posts that levered the stone blocks into their final places. Wooden mallets were used to drive flint wedges into rocks in order to split them. An instrument called an adze, which was similar to what we know today as a wood plane, was employed to give wooden objects the correct finish.

The Egyptians also utilized drills that were fashioned from wood and twine. In order to ensure that the stones were level, wooden rods were joined by strips of twine to check that the surfaces of the stone blocks were flat. Finally, the stone blocks were put onto wooden rockers so that they could more easily be placed into their correct positions on the pyramid.

7. The two tools which were used to place the stones into their final positions on the pyramid were made from which substance?
   A. flint
   B. copper
   C. stone
   D. wood

8. Between paragraphs 1 and 2, the writer's approach shifts from:
   A. scientific explanation to technical analysis
   B. reasoned argument to impassioned persuasion
   C. background information to specific details
   D. personal opinion to justification

9. What is the writer's main purpose?
   A. to give a step-by-step explanation of the construction of the Giza pyramids
   B. to compare the construction of the Giza pyramids to that of modern day structures
   C. to give an overview of some of the main implements that were used to construct the Giza pyramids
   D. to highlight the importance of the achievement of the construction of the Giza pyramids

10. Which of the following assumptions has most influenced the writer?
    A. It is incredible that the Egyptians were able to construct the pyramids using only hand-made tools.
    B. It is a pity that the wheel was not available to the Egyptians during the construction of the pyramids at Giza.
    C. Modern construction projects could learn from the example of the Giza pyramids.
    D. The most difficult aspect of the project was placing the stones in the correct position on the pyramid.

The theory of multiple intelligences (MI) is rapidly replacing the intelligence quotient, or IQ. The IQ, long considered the only valid way of measuring intelligence, has come under criticism recently because it inheres in many cultural biases. For this reason, there has been a movement away from the IQ test, which is now seen as an indication of a person's academic ability. On the other hand, the theory of multiple intelligences measures practical skills such as spatial, visual, and musical ability.

Howard Gardner, the researcher who designed the system of multiple intelligences, posits that while most people have one dominant type of intelligence, most of us have more than one type. Of course, that's why they are known as multiple intelligences. As we will see today, this theory has important implications for teaching and learning.

11. Which of the following groups of statements best summarizes the main topics addressed in each paragraph?
    A. I. Disadvantages of the IQ test; II. The work of Howard Gardner
    B. I. The rise of the theory of multiple intelligences; II. Further information on the theory of multiple intelligences
    C. I. Cultural biases of the IQ test; II. The plurality of multiple intelligences
    D. I. IQ testing and academic performance; II. Dominant types of multiple intelligences

12. The information the writer conveys in this passage is addressed mainly to:
    A. licensed psychologists attending a conference.
    B. college students attending a psychology class.
    C. college students attending an education class.
    D. the general public.

Read Passages 1 and 2 below. Then answer the questions. You need to answer based on ideas that are stated, suggested, or implied in the passage.

Passage 1:

Resulting from the amazing success of WAP (Wireless Application Protocol) in smart phones and hand-held devices, wireless technology can have an amazing impact on your day-to-day life. These technologies helped to make the mobile information society happen by blurring the boundaries between home, the office, and the outside world.

The seamless integration and connectivity that wireless technology brings with it make it possible to work more efficiently. Business users can explore a wide range of interactive services which were difficult to envisage years ago because of the complexity involved in making such devices communicate with each other.

In addition, with wireless technologies, you can get on social media wherever you are, helping us stay connected with friends and family.

Passage 2:

Recent research shows that social media platforms may actually be making us antisocial. Survey results indicate that many people would prefer to interact on Facebook or Instagram, rather than see friends and family in person. The primary reason cited for this phenomenon was that one does not need to go to the effort to dress up and travel in order to use these social media platforms.

Another independent survey revealed that people often remain glued to their hand-held devices when they do go out with friends. It therefore seems that social media platforms may be having a detrimental effect on our social skills and interpersonal relationships.

13. The writer of Passage 1 would most likely criticize the writer of Passage 2 for:
    A. relying on research results rather than anecdotal information.
    B. placing too much emphasis on certain social media platforms.
    C. talking about hand-held devices in particular, rather than wireless technology in general.
    D. overlooking the positive effect that wireless technologies have had on work and office life.

14. The writer of Passage 2 would probably respond to the last sentence in Passage 1 (you can . . . family.) by
    A. asserting that one should try to balance time spent on social media platforms with time spent in person with loved ones.
    B. pointing out that social media platforms are very convenient.
    C. claiming that we are actually damaging relationships with our friends and family in many cases because of wireless technologies.
    D. arguing that people should leave their hand-held devices at home when going out with friends.

15. The writers of both passages would agree that:
    A. wireless technologies have impacted upon society in positive ways.
    B. social media platforms need to be used with caution.
    C. social media platforms have brought about changes to interpersonal relationships.
    D. Facebook and Instagram are useful interactive tools for business users.

Read the passages and then select the correct answers to the questions. You need to answer based on ideas that are stated, suggested, or implied in the passage.

It was the last day of July. The long hot summer was drawing to a close; and we, the weary pilgrims of the London pavement, were beginning to think of the cloud-shadows on the corn-fields, and the autumn breezes on the sea-shore.

For my own poor part, the fading summer left me out of health and out of spirits. During the past year I had not managed my professional resources as carefully as usual; and my extravagance now limited me to the prospect of spending the autumn economically between my mother's cottage at Hampstead and my own chambers in town.

The evening, I remember, was still and cloudy. It was one of the two evenings in every week which I was accustomed to spend with my mother and my sister. So I turned my steps northward in the direction of Hampstead.

The quiet twilight was still trembling on the topmost ridges of the heath; and the view of London below me had sunk into a black gulf in the shadow of the cloudy night, when I stood before the gate of my mother's cottage. I had hardly rung the bell before the house door was opened violently; my worthy Italian friend, Professor Pesca, appeared in the servant's place; and darted out joyously to receive me, with a shrill foreign parody on an English cheer.

I had first become acquainted with my Italian friend by meeting him at certain great houses where he taught his own language and I taught drawing. All I then knew of the history of his life was, that he had once held a situation in the University of Padua; that he had left Italy for political reasons (the nature of which he uniformly declined to mention to any one); and that he had been for many years respectably established in London as a teacher of languages.

I had seen him risk his life in the sea at Brighton. We had met there accidentally, and were bathing together. It never occurred to me that the art which we were practicing might merely add one more to the list of manly exercises which the Professor believed that he could learn impromptu.

16. What does the narrator suggest in paragraph 2?
    A. that he has run out of money
    B. that he has lost all his clients
    C. that he is suffering from depression
    D. that he does not get along well with his mother

17. Why does the narrator mention his mother and sister in paragraph 3?
    A. to imply that Hampstead is in a poorer part of the city
    B. to foreshadow the events that will take place in his mother's cottage
    C. to indicate a routine
    D. to create a contrast with Professor Pesca

18. What is the best paraphrase of the following phrase from paragraph 4?: "appeared in the servant's place."
    A. rang the bell for the doorman
    B. did the job of the doorman
    C. stood where the servant normally stands
    D. received the servant's guests

19. What adjective best describes the narrator's relationship with Professor Pesca?
    A. political
    B. respectable
    C. accidental
    D. collegial

20. What does the narrator state or imply in the last paragraph?
    A. Professor Pesca saved someone who was drowning.
    B. Professor Pesca was not prone to impulsive actions.
    C. Professor Pesca did not know how to swim.
    D. Professor Pesca had experience working with the Coast Guard.

Clare, restless, went out into the dusk when evening drew on, she who had won him having retired to her chamber. The night was as sultry as the day. There was no coolness after dark unless on the grass. Roads, garden-paths, the house-fronts, the bartonwalls were warm as earths, and reflected the noontime temperature into the *noctambulist's* face.

He sat on the east gate of the yard, and knew not what to think of himself. Feeling had indeed smothered judgement that day. Since the sudden embrace, three hours before, the twain had kept apart. She seemed stilled, almost alarmed, at what had occurred, while the novelty, unpremeditation, mastery of circumstance disquieted him—palpitating, contemplative being that he was. He could hardly realize their true relations to each other as yet, and what their mutual bearing should be before third parties thenceforward.

The windows smiled, the door coaxed and beckoned, the creeper blushed confederacy. A personality within it was so far-reaching in her influence as to spread into and make the bricks, mortar, and whole overhanging sky throb with a burning sensibility. Whose was this mighty personality? A milkmaid's.

It was amazing, indeed, to find how great a matter the life of this place had become to him. And though new love was to be held partly responsible for this, it was not solely so. Many have learnt that the magnitude of lives is not as to their external displacements, but as to their subjective experiences. The impressionable peasant leads a larger, fuller, more dramatic life than the king. Looking at it thus, he found that life was to be seen of the same magnitude here as elsewhere.

Despite his heterodoxy, faults, and weaknesses, Clare was a man with a conscience. Tess was no insignificant creature to toy with and dismiss; but a woman living her precious life—a life which, to herself who endured or enjoyed it, possessed as great a dimension as the life of the mightiest to himself. Upon her sensations the whole world depended to Tess; through her existence all her fellow-creatures existed, to her. The universe itself only came into being for Tess on the particular day in the particular year in which she was born.

21. The bartonwalls mentioned in paragraph 1 are most likely:
    A. an area in the garden.
    B. a feature of the natural landscape.
    C. a part of the house.
    D. a path leading to one of the roads.

22. What is the meaning of the word "noctambulist" as it is used in paragraph 1?
    A. a person who suddenly falls in love
    B. a person who responds impulsively to subjective experiences
    C. a person who experiences an external displacement
    D. a person who goes for a walk after dark

23. What is the best paraphrase of the following statement from paragraph 2: "what their mutual bearing should be before third parties thenceforward"?
    A. how they should behave to each other around other people
    B. whether or not they should support each other as a couple from this moment onwards
    C. whether or not they should kiss each other in public
    D. how they should decide whom to tell that they are now a couple

24. Where does the story take place?
    A. in a royal court
    B. in a peasant's abode
    C. in a dairy farm
    D. in a manor house

25. What does the narrator imply when he states that "Clare was a man with a conscience"?
    A. Clare has behaved poorly towards women in the past, but he repents of this behavior.
    B. Clare knows that Tess is hypersensitive, but she has to be aware of his needs.
    C. Clare understands that his life in his current environment may not be of the same magnitude that he has experienced in the past.
    D. Clare realizes that he needs to treat Tess well because she has had her own life experiences, both positive and negative.

EXTENDED READING PRACTICE SET 1

[1] The question of the mechanics of motion is complex and one that has a protracted history. Indeed, much has been discovered about gravity, defined as the force that draws objects to the earth, both before and since the British mathematician Sir Isaac Newton mused upon the subject in the 17th century. As early as the third century B.C., a Greek philosopher and natural scientist named Aristotle conducted a great deal of scientific investigation into the subject. Most of Aristotle's life was devoted to the study of the objects of natural science, and it is for this work that he is most renowned. The Greek scientist wrote a tome entitled *Metaphysics*, which contains the observations that he made as a result of performing this original research in the natural sciences.

[2] Several centuries later, in the first century AD, Ptolemy, another Greek scientist, was credited with a **nascent**, yet unformulated theory, that there was a force that moved toward the center of the earth, thereby holding objects on its surface. Although later ridiculed for his belief that the earth was the center of the planetary system, **Aristotle's compatriot** nevertheless did contribute to the development of the theory of gravity. {A *}

[3] However, it was during the period called the Renaissance that gravitational forces were perhaps studied most widely. An astronomer, Galileo Galilei corrected one of Aristotle's erring theories by pointing out that objects of differing weights fall to earth at the same speed. Years later, Descartes, who was known at that time as a dilettante philosopher, but was later dubbed the father of modern mathematics, held that a body in circular motion constantly strives to recede from the center. This theory gave credence to the notion that bodies in motion had their own forces.

[4] Newton took these studies a step further, and used them to show that the earth's rotation does not fling bodies into the air because the force of gravity, measured by the rate of falling bodies, is greater than the centrifugal force arising from the rotation. In his first mathematical formulation of gravity, published in 1687, Newton posited that the same force that kept the moon from being propelled away from the earth also applied to gravity at the earth's surface. {B *} While this finding, termed the Law of Universal Gravitation, is said to have been occasioned by Newton's observation of the fall of an apple from a tree in the orchard at his home, in reality, the idea did not come to the scientist in a flash of inspiration, but was developed slowly over time.

[5] Newton had the **prescience** to appreciate that his study was of great importance for the scientific community and for society as a whole. It is because of Newton's work that we currently understand the effect of gravity on the earth as a global system. For instance, as a result of Newton's investigation into the subject of gravity, we know today that geological features such as mountains and canyons can cause variances in the Earth's gravitational force. {C *} Newton must also be acknowledged for the realization that the force of gravity becomes less robust as the distance from the equator diminishes, due to the rotation of the earth, as well as the declining mass and density of the planet from the equator to the poles.

[6] In spite of these discoveries, Newton remained perplexed throughout his lifetime by the causes of the power implied by the variables of his mathematical equations on gravity. In other words, he was unable adequately to explain the natural forces upon which the power of gravity relied. Even though he tried to justify these forces by describing them merely as phenomena of nature, differing hypotheses on these phenomena still abound today. {D *}

[7] In 1915, Albert Einstein addressed Newton's reservations by developing the revolutionary theory of general relativity. Einstein asserted that the paths of objects in motion can sometimes deviate, or change direction over the course of time, as a result of the curvature of space time. Numerous subsequent investigations into and tests of the theory of general relativity have unequivocally supported Einstein's groundbreaking work.

1. The word **nascent** in the passage is closest in meaning to:
   A. newly formed
   B. old fashioned
   C. widely accepted
   D. obviously untrue

2. The phrase **Aristotle's compatriot** in paragraph 2 refers to:
   A. *Metaphysics*
   B. the planetary system
   C. Ptolemy
   D. an unformulated theory

3. Which of the sentences below is the best paraphrase of the following sentence from paragraph 4?
   While this finding, termed the Law of Universal Gravitation, is said to have been occasioned by Newton's observation of the fall of an apple from a tree in the orchard at his home, in reality, the idea did not come to the scientist in a flash of inspiration, but was developed slowly over time.
   A. Newton created his Law of Universal Gravitation immediately after he observed an apple falling from a tree in his orchard.
   B. The Law of Universal Gravitation, while similar on occasion to falling apples, is usually the result of observing objects which fall more slowly to earth.
   C. Newton's law of gravity was not the result of a single observation of a fruit tree, but rather was created over many years.
   D. Stories about Newton's observance of falling apples are based on fact, rather than folklore, because of the time-consuming process of the theories relating to these stories.

4. The word **prescience** in the passage is closest in meaning to:
   A. pre-scientific
   B. hindsight
   C. investigation
   D. perception

5. All of the following key facts about gravity are mentioned in paragraph 5 except:
   A. the effect of geology upon gravitational forces
   B. the impact of the varying density of the earth on gravity
   C. the manner in which gravitational force becomes weaker near the equator
   D. the way in which gravity influences rock formations

6. In paragraph 6, what is the author's main purpose?
   A. to emphasize the significance of Newton's achievement
   B. to identify a reservation which Newton experienced
   C. to analyze natural phenomena
   D. to reconcile various gravitational theories

7. Based on the information contained in paragraph 7, which of the following best explains the term "general relativity"?
   A. changes in the motion of objects due to the curved path of space time
   B. the inverse relationship between time and space
   C. the proportionality between paths and objects
   D. the manner in which later researchers supported Einstein

8. Look at the four stars { * } that indicate where the following sentence could be added to the passage:
   Accordingly, an immense amount of research has been devoted to this subject throughout the twentieth and twenty-first centuries.
   What is the correct position for this sentence?
   A. {A*}
   B. {B*}
   C. {C*}
   D. {D*}

9. According to paragraph 7, what can be inferred about the reaction of the scientific community to Einstein's theory of general relativity?
   A. It has received a mixed response.
   B. The response has been overwhelmingly positive.
   C. The reception has been mostly negative.
   D. The scientific community is still undecided about the value of Einstein's work.

10. Select the group of three answers below that represents the most important ideas contained in the passage.
    A. (i) Ptolemy is one of the most famous natural scientists.
       (ii) The strength of gravitational force is directly related to the distance to the equator.
       (iii) Newton was confused by the power from which gravity was derived.
    B. (i) The study of the mechanics of motion has endured for many centuries.
       (ii) Ptolemy is one of the most famous natural scientists.
       (iii) Newton was confused by the power from which gravity was derived.
    C. (i) The study of the mechanics of motion has endured for many centuries.
       (ii) Newton's study of gravitational forces was of invaluable significance.
       (iii) Einstein's theory of general relativity provided much-needed developments to Newton's work.
    D. (i) Ptolemy is one of the most famous natural scientists.
       (ii) The strength of gravitational force is directly related to the distance to the equator.
       (iii) Einstein's theory of general relativity provided much-needed developments to Newton's work.

[1] Socio-economic status plays a key role in a child's success later in life, rather than intellectual ability, according to a recent study. As an example, let's direct our attention to two elementary school students named Paul and John. Both children are attentive and respectful to their teachers, and both earn good grades. However, Paul's father is an affluent property magnate, while John's dad works on an assembly line in a factory. Even though their academic aptitudes are similar, Paul is 30 times more likely than John to have a high-paying career before reaching his fortieth birthday simply due to the differences in the economic situations of their parents. Indeed, statistics reveal that students like John have a 12% chance of finding and keeping jobs that earn only median-level incomes. {A *}

[2] Research dealing with the economics of inequality among adults supports these findings. Importantly, these studies also reveal that the economics of inequality is a trend that has become more and more pronounced in recent years. For instance, in 1960, the **mean** after-tax pay for a U.S. corporate executive was more than 12 times that of the average factory worker. In 1974, the average CEO's pay had increased to nearly 35 times that of a typical blue-collar worker. By 1980, the situation was even worse: the executive's wages and benefits were nearly 42 times that of the average wage of a factory worker. In the twenty-first century, this situation reached a level which some economists have called **hyper-inequality**. That is, it is now common for the salary of the average executive to be more than 100 times that of the average factory employee. In fact, in the current year, most CEOs are making, on average, 530 times more than blue-collar employees.

[3] Because of this and other economic dichotomies, a theoretical stance has recently sprung into existence, asserting that inequality is institutionalized. **{B *}** In keeping with this concept, many researchers argue that workers from higher socio-economic backgrounds are disproportionately compensated, even though the contribution they make to society is no more valuable than **that of their lower-paid counterparts**. To rectify the present imbalance caused by this economic **stratification**, researchers claim that economic rewards should be judged by and distributed according to the worthiness of the employment to society as a whole. Economic rewards under this schema refer not only to wages or salaries, but also to power, status, and prestige within one's community, as well as within larger society.

[4] Recently, cultural and critical theorists have joined in the economic debate that empirical researchers embarked upon decades ago. Focusing on the effect of cultural technologies and systems, they state that various forms of media promote the mechanisms of economic manipulation and oppression. Watching television, they claim, causes those of lower socio-economic class to view themselves as apolitical and powerless victims of the capitalistic machine. Of course, such a phenomenon would have a **deleterious** impact upon individual identity and human motivation. **{C *}**

[5] At a more personal level, economic inequality also has pervasive effects on the lives of the less economically fortunate. These personal effects include the manner in which one's economic status influences musical tastes, the perception of time and space, the expression of emotion, and the communication across social groups. The **detrimental** economic imbalance may at its most extreme form lead to differences in health and mortality in those from the lower economic levels of society. **{D *}**

[6] While causing problems to many on a personal level, economic inequality is also of concern from a global perspective. The worldwide impact of economic inequality is so severe at present that certain poorer countries are considered to be peripheral during discussions of international monetary policy. In order to solve this problem, many economists believe that consideration must be given not only to political arrangements that make some groups more financially better off than others, but also to the social interaction between people and groups.

[7] Conversely, other theorists argue that financial improvement does not always result in the betterment of any particular society. They point out that levels of personal happiness, as well as trust and cooperation between people, are often highest when monetary considerations within a group are kept to a minimum. Finally, they warn that judgements about any given nation's financial situation may be biased as a result of the Western emphasis on materialism and consumerism.

11. The word **mean** in the passage is closest in meaning to:
    A. unpleasant
    B. cheap
    C. basic
    D. average

12. Based on the information in paragraph 2, which of the following best explains the term **hyper-inequality**?
    A. The fact that the disparity between high and low level salaries has become so enormous.
    B. The fact that high and low level salaries are bifurcated.
    C. The fact that economists are keenly interested in the subject of financial inequality.
    D. The fact that CEOs have more prestige than factory workers.

13. The word **stratification** in the passage is closest in meaning to:
    A. paid at a low-level
    B. occurring in pairs
    C. divided into levels
    D. divided into steps of a process

14. The words **that of their lower-paid counterparts** in the passage refer to:
    A. the inequality which lower-paid workers encounter
    B. the compensation paid to people of lower-level incomes
    C. the salaries of people from affluent socio-economic strata
    D. the benefit to society from the work of lower compensated people

15. According to paragraph 4, all of the following are accurate statements except:
    A. Cultural theorists have expanded upon the work of previous research.
    B. Television and other media have an effect on social inequality.
    C. Television viewing can reinforce feelings of socio-economic subjugation.
    D. People who view television are more motivated to change their lives.

16. The word **detrimental** in the passage is closest in meaning to:
    A. noisome
    B. advantageous
    C. antisocial
    D. deathly

17. Look at the four stars { * } that indicate where the following sentence could be added to the passage.
    This burgeoning school of thought claims that social structures reinforce economic inequality by attaching more value and prestige to some careers than others.
    What is the correct position for this sentence?
    A. {A *}
    B. {B *}
    C. {C *}
    D. {D *}

18. Which of the sentences below is the best paraphrase of the following sentence from paragraph 6?
    The worldwide impact of economic inequality is so severe at present that certain poorer countries are considered to be peripheral during discussions of international monetary policy.
    A. The influence of poverty has wide-reaching, global implications.
    B. Some countries that are less economically advanced are thought to be irrelevant when debates about worldwide economic protocol take place.
    C. Economic inequality has made certain countries poorer because of debates about international financial matters.
    D. External discussions have increased the severity of worldwide financial inequality.

19. Why does the author mention Paul and John in paragraph 1 of the passage?
    A. To emphasize the needs of blue-collar employees
    B. To portray a tragic situation that has occurred in the past
    C. To illustrate the economic effects of social inequality
    D. To describe how poverty has impacted upon the life of one particular child

20. The word **deleterious** in the passage is closest in meaning to:
    A. motivating
    B. equalizing
    C. injurious
    D. judicious

21. According to the passage, which of the following statements best characterizes the personal effects of economic inequality?
    A. Socio-economic status has wide-ranging effects on life and lifestyle, as well as on a number of personal preferences and behaviors.
    B. Socio-economic level primarily affects communication skills.
    C. Socio-economic unfairness results predominantly in lethargy among those most profoundly affected by it.
    D. Socio-economic inequality usually results in premature death to those who experience it.

22. According to paragraph 6 of the passage, how might the global effects of economic inequality be solved?
    A. by focusing on international political discussions on this problem
    B. by paying attention to the political as well as the social causes of inequality
    C. by heeding the results of various social interactions
    D. by exploring the way in which the political and social aspects of inequality are intertwined

23. Based on the information in paragraph 7, what can be inferred about the present debate on socio-economic inequality?
    A. All theorists agree about the best course of action to take in order to address the issue of economic disparities.
    B. There is unanimous agreement that an improvement in financial conditions leads to an amelioration of other social problems.
    C. There is some dispute surrounding the social and non-monetary effects associated with financial improvement.
    D. Western capitalism serves as the agreed upon, uniform standard towards which all nations should strive.

[1] Jean Piaget is one of the most well-known theorists in child development and educational psychology, and the scholastic community still discusses his principles today. Focusing his research on the processes by which human beings learn how to exist in their environments, Piaget strived to answer the question: "How do human beings obtain knowledge?" He is responsible for discovering what he termed "**abstract symbolic reasoning**." This term refers to the notion that biology impacts upon child development much more than socialization. Piaget determined that younger children responded to research questions differently than older children. His conclusion was that different responses occurred not because younger children were less intelligent, but because they were at a lower level of biological development. {A *}

[2] As a biologist, Piaget had an intense curiosity in the manner in which organisms adapted to their environments, and this interest resulted in several revolutionary theories. Piaget postulated that children's behaviors were regulated by mental structures called "schemes," which enable a child to interpret the world and respond appropriately to new situations. Piaget observed the process by which human beings have to learn how use their mental structures as they become familiarized with their environments, and he **coined** the term "equilibration" to describe this process.

[3] The biologist noted that all children are born with the drive to adapt, and he therefore posited that mental schemes of adaptation are innate. While an animal continues to use its in-born adaptation schemes throughout its entire existence, human beings, in Piaget's view, have innate schemes that compete with and then bifurcate from constructed schemes, which are those that are acquired as one interacts with and adapts to his or her social environment. {B *}

[4] The process of adaptation, which is split into the two distinct functions of assimilation and accommodation, was of paramount importance in Piaget's research. The function of assimilation refers to the way in which a person transforms the environment in order to utilize innate cognitive schemes and structures. Alternatively, the **latter function** is used to describe the way in which pre-existing schemes or mental structures are altered in the process of accepting the conditions of one's environment. For

example, the schemes used in bottle feeding or breast feeding a baby illustrate the process of assimilation because the child utilizes his or her innate ability to for suckle to carry out both tasks. Further, when a child begins to eat with a spoon rather than a bottle, he or she uses accommodation since a completely new way of eating must be learned.

[5] As Piaget's body of research expanded, he identified four developmental stages of cognition in children. In the first stage, which he called the sensorimotor stage, Piaget observed that at the **incipience** of the child's cognitive development, intelligence is demonstrated in the manner in which the infant interacts physically with the world. In other words, intelligence is directly related to mobility and motor activity at this stage. In addition, children start to obtain language skills and memory, which Piaget termed "object permanence," in this initial developmental stage. {C *}

[6] As a toddler, the child begins the pre-operational stage, which is quite **egocentric**, so most of his or her intellectual and emotional energy is self-centered rather than empathetic at this point of development. {D *} Although intelligence, language, and memory continue developing during this time, thinking is mainly inflexible and illogical.

[7] The concrete operational stage begins at approximately age 5. Logical and systematic thought processes appear during this stage, and the child begins to comprehend measurement and symbols pertaining to concrete objects, such as numbers, amounts, volumes, lengths, and weights. The egocentrism of the previous stage begins to diminish during the concrete operational stage as thinking becomes more logical.

[8] The final stage, termed the formal operational stage, begins at the start of the teenage years. This stage is normally characterized by abstract thought on a wide range of complex ideas and theories. However, research has indicated that adults in many countries have not completed this stage due to the lack of educational opportunities or poverty.

24. Based upon paragraph 1, which is the best explanation for the term **abstract symbolic reasoning**?
    A. Older children are more intelligent than younger children.
    B. Older children are more physically developed that younger children.
    C. Older children are more socially developed than younger children.
    D. The intellectual development of children is affected by their biological development.

25. The best synonym for the term **coined** is:
    A. realized
    B. recovered
    C. invented
    D. utilized

26. According to paragraph 2, the following statements about Piaget are true except:
    A. Piaget's work as a biologist had a profound impact upon his research on child development.
    B. Piaget understood that mental development is closely connected to biological development.
    C. Piaget realized that biological factors affected child development, in addition to environmental factors.
    D. Piaget was the very first researcher on the subject of child development.

27. The best synonym for the word **incipience** in the passage is:
    A. start
    B. prime
    C. mental
    D. active

28. The best synonym for the word **egocentric** in the passage is:
    A. shy
    B. selfish
    C. uninformed
    D. illogical

29. Look at the four stars { * } that indicate where the following sentence could be added to the passage.
    Further, as schemes become more complex due to this cycle of interaction and adaptation, they are termed "structures."
    Where is the best place to insert this new sentence?
    A. {A *}
    B. {B *}
    C. {C *}
    D. {D *}

30. Which of the sentences below is the best paraphrase of the following sentence from paragraph 3?
    While an animal continues to use its in-born adaptation schemes throughout its entire existence, human beings, in Piaget's view, have innate schemes that compete with and then bifurcate from constructed schemes, which are those that are acquired as one interacts with and adapts to his or her social environment.
    A. Piaget theorized that, unlike the schemes of other animals, human being's schemes are primarily acquired in the socialization process.
    B. In contrast to other animals, human beings use their innate schemes throughout their lifetimes, rather than departing from constructed schemes.
    C. The process by which human beings acquire schemes is different than that of other animals because human beings acquire schemes during the socialization process, and these acquired schemes diverge from their innate schemes.
    D. Piaget noted that human beings differ to other animals since they do not rely only on in-born cognitive mechanisms.

31. The words the **latter function** in the passage refer to:
    A. assimilation
    B. transformation
    C. conformance
    D. accommodation

32. Why does the author mention bottle feeding in paragraph 4 of the passage?
    A. To identify one of the important features of assimilation
    B. To exemplify the assimilation process
    C. To describe the importance of assimilation
    D. To explain difficulties that children face during assimilation

33. According to the passage, which of the following statements best characterizes the sensorimotor stage?
    A. The growth of the child's intelligence in this stage depends predominantly on his or her verbal ability.
    B. The skills obtained during this stage are of less importance than those achieved during later developmental stages.
    C. During this stage, the child learns how his or her mobility relates to language.
    D. The child's cognitive development in this stage is achieved through physical movement in his or her environment.

34. Based on the information in paragraphs 6 and 7, what can be inferred about child development?
    A. Before the child enters the concrete operational stage, his or her thinking is largely rigid and unsystematic.
    B. The conceptualization of symbols is not as important as the conceptualization of numbers.
    C. The child becomes more egocentric during the concrete operational stage.
    D. Memory and language become less important during the concrete operational stage.

35. According to the passage, the formal operational stage:
    A. is the result of poor economic conditions.
    B. has not yet been finished by many individuals around the world.
    C. is an important global problem.
    D. in no way is connected to the availability of education.

36. What is the author's main purpose?
    A. To provide biographical information about Jean Piaget
    B. To discuss the significant aspects of Jean Piaget's theories on child development
    C. To criticize the research of Jean Piaget
    D. To point out flaws in current child development theory

EXTENDED READING PRACTICE SET 2

[1] Adventurers, fieldwork assistants, and volunteers are gradually replacing tourists. Still, the classification 'tourist' will never totally disappear. There might still be those who wish to travel to foreign lands for their own enjoyment, but doing so will be a **clandestine** and frowned-upon activity. No one will admit to belonging to that category.

[2] Burma and Bali have recently prohibited tourists from entering parts of their countries. The list of places that tourists cannot explore is ever-expanding. The international tourist organization Tourism Concern states that Belize, Botswana, China, East Africa, Peru, Thailand, and Zanzibar all have areas that have been adversely impacted upon by tourism. Representatives from Tourism Concern believe that tourists are destroying the environment, as well as local cultures. These representatives also assert that although tourists bring money to the countries they visit, they must be stopped at any price. **{A *}**

[3] **These notions** may seem ironic since tourism was unquestionably encouraged as something that was inherently good a few decades ago. The advent of relatively less expensive accommodation and flights has meant that tourism can finally be enjoyed by the majority of the population. The United Nations declared the year 1967 "The International Year of the Tourist," and during the twenty-first century, more and more families are traveling abroad on family vacations. **{B *}**

[4] The World Tourism Organization (WTO) has predicted that by the year 2050, there will be 1.56 billion tourists per year traveling somewhere in the world. This forecast demonstrates the immense challenge in trying to curb the global demand for tourism. In fact, the task may be so tremendous that it might just be impossible.

[5] Some argue that the government should intervene, but the government alone would face huge impediments in attempting to make so many economically-empowered people stop doing something that they enjoy. Others assert that tourism is of such extreme damage to the welfare of the world that only totally irresponsible individuals would ever consider doing it. Yet, this argument is clearly **absurd**. Whatever benefits or otherwise accrue from tourism, it is not evil, despite what a tiny minority might say. It can cause harm. It can be neutral, and it can occasionally bring about something good.

[6] As a result, tourism is under attack by more a more oblique method: it has been re-named. Bit by bit, the word "tourist" is being removed from the tourism industry.

[7] Since tourism has changed, so too must the vacation. Adventurers, fieldwork assistants, and volunteers do not go on vacations. These new travelers go on "cultural experiences", "expeditions" or "projects". However, re-branding tourism in this way gives freedom to travelers, as well as restrictions.

[8] The various booklets, pamphlets, and brochures distributed by the new industry for travelers are now attempting to **emulate** advertisements produced by charities. For example, *Global Adventure* magazine produces an annual "99 Great Adventures Guide" which mixes charitable expeditions with vacations as if the two things are one and the same.

[9] New travelers express great interest in respecting the environments they visit. They avoid **tourist infrastructures** because they are afraid of being viewed negatively by the local culture. Instead, they prefer accommodation arrangements such as cabins or camping. These types of accommodation, they believe, are more respectful of local culture. Local culture is very important to the new tourist, whereas the mass tourist is believed to destroy it. **{C *}**

[10] Nevertheless, all types of tourism should be responsible towards and respectful of environmental and human resources. Some tourism developers, as well as individual tourists, have not acted with this in mind. Consequently, a divide is being driven between those few **affluent** and privileged tourists and the remaining majority. **{D *}**

1. What is the best title for this passage?
    A. Tourism and the Environment
    B. Adventurers, Tourists, and Travelers
    C. The Changing Face of Tourism
    D. Tourism: Its Advantages and Disadvantages

2. The word **clandestine** in the passage is closest in meaning to:
    A. distressing
    B. secret
    C. pleasurable
    D. difficult

3. The author mentions all off the following facts about tourism in paragraphs 2 and 3 except:
    A. the names of certain countries that have banned tourists.
    B. the names of countries that have been negatively affected by tourism.
    C. the reasons why flights became inexpensive.
    D. the reasons why new views on tourism may seem paradoxical when compared to views on tourism in the past.

4. The word **absurd** in the passage is closest in meaning to:
    A. ridiculous
    B. beneficial
    C. proper
    D. damaging

5. The word **emulate** in the passage is closest in meaning to:
    A. strive
    B. utilize
    C. imitate
    D. distribute

6. Look at the four stars { * } that indicate where the following sentence could be added to the passage.
    Our concern should be not with this small number of privileged people, but rather with the majority of travelers.
    Where is the best place to insert this new sentence?
    A. {A *}
    B. {B *}
    C. {C *}
    D. {D *}

7. Which of the sentences below is the best paraphrase of the following sentence from paragraph 5?
    Whatever benefits or otherwise accrue from tourism, it is not evil, despite what a tiny minority might say.
    A. Although the benefits of tourism may be questionable, tourism is not morally wrong, in spite of what a few detractors might believe.
    B. Even though some people may believe tourism is wicked, it is not really wrong because of its obvious benefits.
    C. Tourism should not be stopped, in spite of some disadvantages, because it may be beneficial to the minority.
    D. In spite of what a few people believe, very few benefits result from tourism.

8. Based on the information in paragraph 9, which of the following best explains the term **tourist infrastructures**?
    A. Hotels and other physical structures that have been purpose-built for tourists.
    B. New campgrounds and cabins that have been erected for tourists.
    C. Buildings and other physical structures that show respect for the local environment.
    D. Any structure that lessens the divide between tourism and the local culture.

9. The words **these notions** in the passage refer to:
    A. The way that tourists bring money to the countries they visit.
    B. The manner in which tourism helps local cultures.
    C. The fact that tourism used to be encouraged as something good.
    D. The viewpoints that express disdain for tourism.

10. Why does the author mention "cultural experiences," "expeditions," or "projects" in paragraph 7 of the passage?
    A. To exemplify how tourists respect the environment
    B. To contradict the evidence in support of advertising
    C. To illustrate how tourism has been re-branded
    D. To argue that charitable expeditions are now indistinguishable from vacations

11. According to the passage, which of the following examples best characterizes how tourists can be more respectful of their environments?
    A. By avoiding the local culture
    B. By using unconventional types of lodging arrangements
    C. By viewing the local culture in an unbiased way
    D. By emphasizing the disadvantages of mass tourism

12. The word **affluent** in the passage is closest in meaning to:
    A. obnoxious
    B. detrimental
    C. oblivious
    D. wealthy

13. Which of the following best expresses the author's attitude towards the past effects of tourism on the environment?
    A. regrettable
    B. capricious
    C. unclear
    D. uncertain

[1] Every morning, tens of thousands of children under age ten have nothing to eat or drink before leaving home for school. Research also shows that out of all youths in the 13-year-old age group, 7% are regular smokers. In addition, the consumption of alcoholic beverages in the 11-to-15-year-old age group has more than doubled in the past decade, with 25% of this age group drinking on average the equivalent of over four cans of beer every week.

[2] In spite of an overall trend for improvements in child health, inequalities in health have been on the rise. A significant aspect of **health inequalities** is that rates of disease and death are far higher in poorer households. One key reason for **tackling** the issue of child poverty is to rectify in particular the inequalities in child health, which will otherwise carry over into adulthood. Accordingly, the government has made the commitment to attempt to lower child poverty dramatically in the next two decades. {A *}

[3] But will the government's commitment actually reduce child poverty and improve child health? **Cynics** say that the government's monetary support for poor households will invariably be spent on consumables like candy and potato chips, or other junk food, or worse, on tobacco, alcohol, and even drugs. {B *} Realistically, however, providing households with more money in the form of governmental assistance should give them the opportunity to spend more money on nutritious, often more expensive, food.

[4] Yet, if the government truly wishes to improve the health of poor children, it should realize that families cannot rely on only modest increases in income. For the children leaving home without any breakfast, these government measures are not enough. A better option would be to feed **these children** through school breakfast and dinner programs. {C *}

[5] In fact, research demonstrates that children's concentration and learning suffer when they do not have a nutritious breakfast. In response to this research, some countries have developed programs for nutritious school breakfasts and dinners, and **they** have allocated more funds to these meal programs than to welfare benefits. {D *} There remains a clear need for the authorities to address nutrition as one of the worst symptoms of child poverty since disadvantaged children in many areas still do not get a nourishing breakfast and the effectiveness of their education is jeopardized as a result.

[6] Smoking also greatly damages the health of children and increases childhood mortality rates. While the government has raised the cigarette tax, thereby increasing the cost of tobacco to consumers, this has not brought about the desired result. On the contrary, it has left poor parents who smoke worse off, and their children will continue to suffer. Children's health would be better served if the government allocated funds to preventing cigarette sales to children, instead of the hefty monetary resources spent on attempting to halt cigarette smuggling and related tax evasion.

[7] Children, particularly young adolescents, are also sickly because of the ever-increasing consumption of alcohol in this age group. One reason for the rise in children's drinking is the increase in the availability of sweetened bottled alcoholic drinks. These beverages make alcohol more attractive and more **palatable** to young people and children. Nevertheless, the government appears be in something of a quandary, perhaps wishing to speak out against major beverage manufacturing companies, and yet succumbing to lobbying by and accepting related financial support from big businesses like Anheuser-Busch.

[8] Improving children's opportunities depends on ending child poverty and improving the health of the poorest children. While these goals are related, it would be foolish to believe that the reduction of child poverty would automatically improve children's nutrition and reduce their smoking and drinking. Re-thinking the allocation of governmental funds to nutrition and effective education and prevention about addiction are still needed in order to improve child health.

14. According to paragraph 1, the following statements are true except:
    A. Many young children regularly go to school on an empty stomach.
    B. Alcohol consumption has risen across many age groups in the last ten years.
    C. Children as young as thirteen years old have developed smoking habits.
    D. Twenty-five percent of a certain age group regularly consumes alcohol every week.

15. The best definition for the word **tackling** in the passage is:
    A. trying to solve
    B. attempting to analyze
    C. understanding the trends
    D. committing to change

16. Based upon paragraph 2, which is the best explanation of the term **health inequalities**?
    A. Poor children are often hungry and undernourished.
    B. There has been an increased trend for improvements in child health.
    C. Mortality and illness rates are greater for members of poor families.
    D. The government has made a commitment to solving the problems of the poorest children.

17. The best synonym for the word **cynics** in the passage is:
    A. officials
    B. consumers
    C. advisers
    D. doubters

18. Look at the four stars { * } that indicate where the following sentence could be added to the passage.
    Giving free school meals to children from lower-income families would be the best and most direct way of improving child nutrition.
    Where is the best place to insert this new sentence?
    A. {A *}
    B. {B *}
    C. {C *}
    D. {D *}

19. The word **they** highlighted in paragraph 5 refers to:
    A. countries that have established school breakfasts.
    B. children who regularly do not receive breakfast.
    C. researchers in the field of child nutrition.
    D. fund-raisers for school meal programs.

20. Which of the sentences below is the best paraphrase of the following sentence from paragraph 5?
    There remains a clear need for the authorities to address nutrition as one of the worst symptoms of child poverty since disadvantaged children in many areas still do not get a nourishing breakfast and the effectiveness of their education is jeopardized as a result.

    A. The government needs to provide nourishing breakfasts to children so that they can improve their learning.
    B. Poor children do not start the day with a good meal and cannot learn well as a result, so it is of the utmost importance for the government to improve child poverty and child nutrition.
    C. Child poverty continues to be a grave social problem and nutrition is a concomitant issue; therefore, the government should get involved.
    D. Poor nutrition is one aspect of poverty and increased government funds need to be set aside to deal with this situation.

21. Why does the author discuss smoking in paragraph 6 of the passage?
    A. To establish the link between cigarette smuggling and tax evasion
    B. To exemplify how poor parents who smoke will continue to do so, exacerbating their children's health problems
    C. To enumerate details about a government policy
    D. To expand on another aspect of poor health in children

22. According to the passage, what was the main reason for the government's increase in the cigarette tax?
    A. To reduce childhood death rates
    B. To decrease tax evasion relating to tobacco products
    C. To attempt to deter smoking, particularly by poor parents
    D. To impede cigarette smuggling

23. The best synonym for the word **palatable** in the passage is:
    A. acceptable
    B. tasty
    C. desirable
    D. pleasant

24. Based on the information in paragraph 7, what can be inferred about the government's reluctance to criticize the practices of big businesses?
    A. It is loath to lose the monetary support that large beverage companies have to offer.
    B. It realizes that there is no reason to reduce the demand for certain alcoholic drinks.
    C. It wishes to reduce its reliance on financing from lobbyists.
    D. It understands that doing so would not make alcohol less attractive to youngsters.

25. Based on the information in paragraph 8, which statement best describes the relationship between the goals of improved opportunities for children and the problems of child poverty and ill health?
    A. The reduction of governmental reliance on large companies is inextricably intertwined with the goal of improving children's opportunities.
    B. The government needs to re-evaluate its relationship to lobbyists if it is ever going to solve the issue of poor child health.
    C. Establishing the goal of addressing of child poverty will dramatically improve children's health and opportunities, but it may take an extended time period to do so.
    D. The achievement of the goal of the reduction of child poverty would improve child health and increase the opportunities of children to some extent, but it would not entirely eradicate the problem.

26. What is the author's main purpose in this passage?
    A. To decry poor child health and point the finger at the primary culprits
    B. To demonstrate that child health would automatically improve if certain solutions were to be carried out
    C. To enumerate the reasons for health inequalities, particularly in children, and to allude to some possible courses of action
    D. To demonstrate the reasons why the consumption of alcohol and tobacco are harmful for children

[1] Results of a survey on social trends have identified a rise in immigration as the most significant social change in recent years. Homegrown population increases, defined as the surplus of births over deaths, have been surpassed by immigration. In other words, immigration has increased, while natural population growth has fallen. Specifically, at the end of the twentieth century, net inward migration increased, while natural population growth fell. This amounted to a shift in the significance of immigration to changes in the population, with consequences for ethnic mix and structure. Population patterns have changed dramatically as immigration has become the main **catalyst** for population growth. Moreover, migration patterns within the country appear to be closely linked to where and how people choose to live.

[2] In spite of **this steady influx** of new members of the population, most people regard immigration as a very good thing which benefits the country. These benefits include the skills brought by workers that are needed to expand the information technology industry. The younger age profile of immigrants also helps to balance the pressures of an aging population. {A *}

[3] The survey also revealed other important social trends relating to immigration and population. Notably, the population tripled from almost 76 million at the beginning of the twentieth century to nearly 281 million at the start of the twenty-first century. {B *} Average household size declined by 2 people per household over the last century, from 4.6 people per household a hundred years ago to 2.6 members per household today. Population density has increased two-fold during the last one hundred years, but remains relatively low in comparison to most other countries in the world. Alaska had the lowest population density, and the population density of the Northeast, which has always been high, continued consistently to **outstrip** that of other regional areas. While most of the population lived outside cities prior to the end of World War II, the percentage of the population living in metropolitan areas increased in every subsequent decade of the study. New York and California had the largest populations, and Florida and Arizona had the fastest-growing populations during the period of the study. {C *}

[4] Until 1970, the majority of households were living in the Northeast and Midwest, but since 1980, the majority was in the South and West. Slightly more than half of all households are now maintained by people aged 45 and over. Female householders have increased as a proportion of all householders, and older females were far more likely to live alone than were men or younger women. {D *} The per capita marriage rate has fallen in the last fifteen years, and there was a concurrent drop in the per capita divorce rate during this time.

[5] The survey also examined changes to overall national income, as well as the spending habits of individuals and households. It has found that the distribution of income has become more and more unequal over the past forty years, with the income of the richest 10% of the people in the country rising disproportionately to that of the poorest sector of the population. As relatively worse-off households struggle to make essential purchases, the amount of consumer credit has increased to over a trillion dollars, with credit cards and revolving credit arrangements constituting the **lion's share of** this figure. Cash transactions fell sharply as innovative technologies and new forms of payment appeared in the marketplace.

27. The word **catalyst** in this passage is closest in meaning to:
    A. resource
    B. reference
    C. reason
    D. result

28. The words **this steady influx** in this passage refer to:
    A. the consistent improvement in ethnic diversity in the population.
    B. the constant increase in people coming to the country for the first time.
    C. the continual stream of benefits and skills brought by new workers.
    D. the gradual expansion in the technology sector.

29. According to paragraph 3, what was the most notable change to the population in the last one hundred years?
    A. The three-fold increase in the size of the population
    B. The increase in average household size
    C. The worryingly high rise in population density
    D. The low population density in Alaska

30. Look at the four stars { * } that indicate where the following sentence could be added to the passage.
    There was also a dramatic decline in the number of households with 5 or more members and a significant increase the number of one and two-person households.
    What is the correct position for this sentence?
    A.   {A *}
    B.   {B *}
    C.   {C *}
    D.   {D *}

31. The word **outstrip** in this passage is closest in meaning to:
    A.   overwhelm
    B.   compare to
    C.   diminish
    D.   exceed

32. Why does the author mention the changes to the populations of Florida and Arizona?
    A.   To point out that new residents are continually moving to these states
    B.   To contrast their population changes to those in New York and California
    C.   To exemplify the increase in the percentage of the population living in metropolitan areas
    D.   To illustrate why people wish to leave the Northeast and Midwest

33. The phrase **lion's share of** in this passage is closest in meaning to:
    A.   background to
    B.   indebtedness to
    C.   majority of
    D.   fluctuating part of

34. Which of the following statements expresses a possible interpretation of the relationship between the changes to the marriage rate and divorce rate?
    A.   The marriage rate went down because more women preferred to live alone.
    B.   The divorce rate went down because fewer people got married during the period of the study.
    C.   The marriage rated went down because the core of the population is aging.
    D.   The divorce rate declined because existing marriages became more stable.

35. According to paragraph 4, the most notable demographic shift when comparing geographic areas was that:
    A.   Female householders rose as a percentage of all householders.
    B.   Older females live alone more often than do men or younger women.
    C.   The population rose sharply in California and New York over the course of the study.
    D.   Many people moved from the Northeast and Midwest to live in the South or West.

36. Based on the information contained in the passage, what could be inferred about the reason why female householders increased as a proportion of all householders?
    A.   Women are preoccupied about the needs of their children, so they deprioritize other relationships.
    B.   Women generally suffer from a decline in household income after the breakup of a relationship.
    C.   Women are more likely to live alone after losing a life partner than men are.
    D.   The social stigma of divorce is greater for women than men.

37. Summarize the passage by selecting the group of sentences below that express the three most important ideas contained in the passage:
   A.   (i) The population has increased as a result of immigration.
        (ii) There were notable changes in the concentration of the population in certain states and geographic regions.
        (iii) The distribution of income has become increasingly skewed in favor of the rich.
   B.   (i) The population has increased due to increased birth rates and rising immigration.
        (ii) There were notable changes in the concentration of the population in certain states and geographic regions.
        (iii) The distribution of income has become increasingly skewed in favor of the rich.
   C.   (i) There were notable changes in the concentration of the population in certain states and geographic regions.
        (ii) Marriage and divorce rates have fallen.
        (iii) The distribution of income has become increasingly skewed in favor of the rich.
   D.   (i) There were notable changes in the concentration of the population in certain states and geographic regions.
        (ii) The distribution of income has become increasingly skewed in favor of the rich.
        (iii) More and more women prefer to live alone.

English Language Skills Section

Grammar Guide

The sections in the following part of the study guide are intended as an overview of the aspects of grammar most commonly tested on the exam. Read each section carefully, paying special attention to the examples. Then take the practice writing tests that follow.

Adverb Placement

Adverbs are words that express how an action was done. Adverbs often end in the suffix –ly. You can vary adverb placement, depending upon what you want to emphasize in your sentence. Be sure to place the adverb in the correct position in the sentence and to use the comma, if necessary. If the adverb is used as the first word in a sentence, the adverb should be followed by a comma.

    CORRECT: Normally, an economic crisis is a valid reason to raise interest rates.

    CORRECT: An economic crisis is normally a valid reason to raise interest rates.

    INCORRECT: An economic crisis is a valid reason to normally raise interest rates.

Remember not to place an adverb between "to" and the verb, as in the last example above. This practice, known as the split infinitive, is grammatically incorrect.

Commonly-Confused Words

Be careful with the following commonly-confused words:

- adverse (adjective – detrimental) / averse (adjective – reluctant)
- affect (verb – to cause) / effect (noun – the result or outcome)
- allude (imply) / elude (evade)
- allusion (implication) / illusion (appearance)
- bare (verb – to expose) / bear (verb – to take on a burden)
- bale (noun – a cubed package) / bail (verb – to get something out of something else)
- pore (verb – to study or read with care) / pour (verb – to emit or flow)
- principal (adjective – main or predominant)/ principle (noun – a concept)

Now look at the following examples.

    CORRECT: Failure to study will <u>affect</u> your grades.

    INCORRECT: Failure to study will <u>effect</u> your grades.

    CORRECT: A scientific <u>principle</u> is a concise statement about the relationship of one object to another.

    INCORRECT: A scientific <u>principal</u> is a concise statement about the relationship of one object to another.

    CORRECT: The run-away thief <u>eluded</u> the police officer.

    INCORRECT: The run-away thief <u>alluded</u> the police officer.

CORRECT: He thought he saw an oasis in the desert, but it was an optical <u>illusion</u>.

INCORRECT: He thought he saw an oasis in the desert, but it was an optical <u>allusion</u>.

CORRECT: I was depending on her help, but she <u>bailed</u> out at the last minute.

INCORRECT: I was depending on her help, but she <u>baled</u> out at the last minute.

CORRECT: He <u>pored</u> over the book as he studied for the exam.

INCORRECT: He <u>poured</u> over the book as he studied for the exam.

CORRECT: She is <u>averse</u> to receiving help with the project.

INCORRECT: She is <u>adverse</u> to receiving help with the project.

CORRECT: He could not <u>bear</u> to listen to the loud music.

INCORRECT: He could not <u>bare</u> to listen to the loud music.

Misplaced Modifiers

Modifiers are descriptive phrases. The modifier should always be placed directly before or after the noun to which it relates. Now look at the examples.

CORRECT: Like Montana, Wyoming is not very densely populated.

INCORRECT: Like Montana, there isn't a large population in Wyoming.

The phrase "like Montana" is an adjectival phrase that describes or modifies the noun "Wyoming." Therefore, "Wyoming" must come directly after the comma.

Here are two more examples:

CORRECT: While waiting at the bus stop, a senior citizen was mugged.

INCORRECT: While waiting at the bus stop, a mugging took place.

The adverbial phrase "while waiting at the bus stop" modifies the noun phrase "a senior citizen," so this noun phrase needs to come after the adverbial phrase.

Parallel Structure

Correct parallel structure is also known as parallelism. In order to follow the grammatical rules of parallelism, you must be sure that all of the items you give in a series are of the same part of speech. So, all of the items must be nouns or verbs, for example. In other words, you should not use both nouns and verbs in a list. Where verbs are used, they should be in the same form or tense.

CORRECT: The vacation gave me a great chance to unwind, have fun, and experience some excitement. (*Unwind*, *have*, and *experience* are all verbs.)

INCORRECT: The vacation gave me a great chance to unwind, and was fun and quite exciting.

CORRECT: I went jet-skiing, surfing, and snorkeling on our vacation. (*Skiing*, *surfing*, and *snorkeling* are all in the –ing form.)

INCORRECT: I went jet-skiing, surfing, and also snorkeled on our vacation.

CORRECT: The hotel was elegant, comfortable, and modern. (*Elegant*, *comfortable*, and *modern* are all adjectives.)

INCORRECT: The hotel was elegant, comfortable, and had up-to-date facilities.

CORRECT: I enjoyed our hotel room, relaxed in the spa, and ate some truly delicious food on our vacation. (*Enjoyed*, *relaxed*, and *ate* are all verbs in the past simple tense.)

INCORRECT: I enjoyed our hotel room, relaxed in the spa, and the food was truly delicious on our vacation.

Pronoun-Antecedent Agreement

Pronouns are words like the following: he, she, it, they, and them. An antecedent is a phrase that precedes the pronoun in the sentence. Pronouns must agree with their antecedents, so use singular pronouns with singular antecedents and plural pronouns with plural antecedents. Be careful not to mix singular and plural forms.

CORRECT: Each student needs to bring his or her identification to the placement test.

INCORRECT: Each student needs to bring their identification to the placement test.

The antecedent "each student" is singular, so the singular pronouns "his" or "her" should follow this antecedent.

CORRECT: The group lost its enthusiasm for the project.

INCORRECT: The group lost their enthusiasm for the project.

The preceding sentence is incorrect because the antecedent is "group," which is singular, while "their" is plural.

Pronoun Usage – Correct Use of *Its* and *It's*

"Its" is a possessive pronoun, while "it's" is a contraction of "it is".

CORRECT: It's high time you started to study.

INCORRECT: Its high time you started to study.

The sentence could also be stated as follows: It is high time you started to study.

Since the contracted form of "it is" can be used in the alternative sentence above, "it's" is the correct form.

CORRECT: A snake sheds its skin at least once a year.

INCORRECT: A snake sheds it's skin at least once a year.

"Its" is a possessive pronoun referring to the snake, so the apostrophe should not be used.

Pronoun Usage – Demonstrative Pronouns

Demonstrative pronouns include the following words: this, that, these, those

"This" is used for a singular item that is nearby. "That" is used for singular items that are farther away in time or space.

> SINGULAR: This book that I have here is really interesting.
>
> PLURAL: That book on the table over there is really interesting.

"These" is used for plural items that are nearby. "Those" is used for plural items that are farther away in time or space.

> SINGULAR: These pictures in my purse were taken on our vacation.
>
> PLURAL: Those pictures on the wall were taken on our vacation.

Avoid using "them" instead of "those":

> INCORRECT: Them pictures on the wall were taken on our vacation.

Pronoun Usage – Relative Pronouns

Relative pronouns include the following: which, that, who, whom, whose

"Which" and "that" are used to describe things, and "who" and "whom" are used to describe people. "Whose" is used for people or things.

> WHICH: Last night, I watched a romantic-comedy movie which was really funny.
>
> THAT: Last night, I watched a romantic-comedy movie that was really funny.
>
> WHO: Susan always remains calm under pressure, unlike Tom, who is always so nervous.

"Who" is used because we are describing the person. This is known as the nominative case.

> WHOM: To whom should the report be given?

"Whom" is used because the person is receiving an action, which in this case is receiving the report. This is known as the accusative case.

> WHOSE: I went out for lunch with Marta, whose parents are from Costa Rica.
>
> WHOSE: I went out for lunch yesterday at that new restaurant, whose name I don't remember.

Please be sure to look at the section entitled "Restrictive and Non-restrictive Modifiers" for information on how to use punctuation with relative pronouns.

Proper Nouns and Proper Adjectives – Capitalization

Proper nouns state the names of specific people, places, ideas, or things. The names of people, countries, states, buildings, streets, rivers, oceans, countries, companies, and institutions are proper nouns. Be careful not to confuse common nouns and proper nouns. Proper adjectives are derived from proper nouns, so they refer to unique classes of people, places, or things. Proper nouns and adjectives should be capitalized. Look at the capitalization in the following examples.

>CORRECT: A famous American landmark, the geyser named Old Faithful is located in Yellowstone Park in the northwest corner of the state of Wyoming. (*American* is a proper adjective. *Old Faithful*, *Yellowstone Park*, and *Wyoming* are proper nouns.)

>INCORRECT: A famous american landmark, the geyser named old faithful is located in yellowstone park in the Northwest corner of the State of wyoming.

Punctuation – Using the Apostrophe for Possessive Forms

Apostrophe placement depends upon whether a word is singular or plural.

For the singular, the apostrophe should be placed before the letter "s."

>SINGULAR: Our team's performance was poor at the game last night.

For the plural form, the apostrophe should be placed after the letter "s."

>PLURAL: Both teams' performances were poor at the game last night.

Remember that the apostrophe is used in sentences like those above in order to show possession. Also remember not to use the apostrophe unnecessarily.

>INCORRECT: The date's for the events are June 22 and July 5.

>INCORRECT: The dates' for the events are June 22 and July 5.

Punctuation – Using Colons and Semicolons

Colons (:) should be used when giving a list of items. Semicolons (;) should be used to join independent clauses.

>COLON: The shop is offering discounts on the following items: DVDs, books, and magazines.

>SEMICOLON: I thought I would live in this city forever; then I lost my job.

Note that the word following the semicolon should not be capitalized.

Please see the section entitled "Punctuation and Independent Clauses" for more information on joining clauses.

Punctuation – Using Commas with Dates and Locations

Commas should be used after the date and year in dates. Commas should also be used after towns and states.

DATES: On July 4, 1776, the Declaration of Independence was signed.

LOCATIONS: Located in Seattle, Washington, the Space Needle is a major landmark.

Punctuation – Using Commas for Items in a Series

When using "and" and "or" for more than two items in a series, be sure to use the comma before the words "and" and "or."

CORRECT: You need to bring a tent, sleeping bag, and flashlight.

INCORRECT: You need to bring a tent, sleeping bag and flashlight.

Notice the use of the comma after the word "bag" and before the word "and" in the series.

CORRECT: Students can call, write a letter, or send an email.

INCORRECT: Students can call, write a letter or send an email.

Notice the use of the comma after the word "letter" and before the word "or" in the series.

Punctuation and Independent Clauses – Avoiding Run-On Sentences

Run-on sentences are those that use commas to join independent clauses together, instead of correctly using the period.

Because they incorrectly use the comma to fuse sentences together, run-on sentences are sometimes called comma splices.

An independent clause contains a grammatical subject and verb. It therefore can stand alone as its own sentence.

The first word of the independent clause should begin with a capital letter, and the clause should be preceded by a period.

CORRECT: I thought I would live in this city forever. Then I lost my job.

INCORRECT: I thought I would live in this city forever, then I lost my job.

"Then I lost my job" is a complete sentence. It has a grammatical subject (I) and a verb (lost).

The independent clause must be preceded by a period, and the first word of the new sentence must begin with a capital letter.

Alternatively, an appropriate conjunction can be used to join the independent clauses:

CORRECT: I thought I would live in this city forever, and then I lost my job.

Restrictive and Non-restrictive Modifiers

Restrictive modifiers are clauses or phrases that provide essential information in order to identify the grammatical subject. Restrictive modifiers should not be preceded by a comma.

CORRECT: My sister who lives in Indianapolis is a good swimmer. (The speaker has more than one sister.)

In this case, the speaker has more than one sister, and she is identifying which sister she is talking about by giving the essential information "who lives in Indianapolis."

On the other hand, a non-restrictive modifier is a clause or phrase that provides extra information about a grammatical subject in a sentence. A non-restrictive modifier must be preceded by a comma. Non-restrictive modifiers are also known as non-essential modifiers.

CORRECT: My sister, who lives in Indianapolis, is a good swimmer. (The speaker has only one sister.)

In this case, the speaker has only one sister. Therefore, the information about her sister's city of residence is not essential in order to identify which sister she is talking about. The words "who lives in Indianapolis" form a non-restrictive modifier.

Sentence Fragments

A sentence fragment is a group of words that does not express a complete train of thought.

CORRECT: I like Denver because it has a great university.

INCORRECT: I like Denver. Because it has a great university.

In the second example, "because it has a great university" is not a complete thought. This idea needs to be joined with the previous clause in order to be grammatically correct.

Subject-Verb Agreement

For questions on subject-verb agreement, you need to be sure that subjects agree with verbs in number. In other words, use a singular verb with a singular subject and a plural verb with a plural subject. While this sounds straightforward, complications can arise with certain words like "each," "every," "neither," and "either," all of which are in fact singular. Subject-verb agreement can also be confusing when there are intervening words in a sentence.

CORRECT: The flowers in the pots in the garden grow quickly.

INCORRECT: The flowers in the pots in the garden grows quickly.

The grammatical subject in the above sentence is "flowers," not "garden," so the plural form of the verb (*grow*) needs to be used.

CORRECT: Each person in the groups of students needs to pay attention to the instructions.

INCORRECT: Each person in the groups of students need to pay attention to the instructions.

The grammatical subject in the above sentence is "each person," not "students." "Each" is singular and therefore requires the singular form of the verb (*needs*).

CORRECT: Each of the men is very strong and determined.

INCORRECT: Every one of the books are on the shelf.

Subordination

Subordinators include words and phrases such as "although," "but," "even though," "because of," and "due to." Be careful to use commas correctly when subordinating sentences.

CORRECT: I was going to study this evening, but the noise next door made it impossible.

INCORRECT: I was going to study this evening but the noise next door made it impossible.

CORRECT: Although I was going to study this evening, the noise next door made it impossible.

INCORRECT: Although I was going to study this evening the noise next door made it impossible.

The word "but" is a subordinator. Subordinators need to be preceded by a comma, so the first sentence is correct as written.

You also need to use a comma in the middle of the sentence when beginning the sentence with the subordinator.

Review of Verb Tenses:

Present simple tense

The present simple tense is used for habitual actions.

> Example: He *goes* to the office at 8:00 every morning.

The present tense is also used to state scientific truths, facts, and generalizations.

> Example: Water *freezes* at zero degrees Celsius.

Past simple tense

The past simple tense is used for actions that were started and completed in the past.

> Example: I walked three miles yesterday.

Present perfect tense

The present perfect tense is used for actions that were completed in the past, but that have relevancy in the present time.

> Example: I *have studied* every day this week.

The phrase "this week" shows that the action has relevancy in the present time.

Past perfect tense

The past perfect tense is used for an action that was completed in the past, prior to another action that was completed in the past.

> Example: We had just sent the letter when the email arrived.

Passive tenses

Use the passive voice to emphasize the object of the action, rather than the person who was conducting the action.

In the example sentence that follows in this section, the diplomas are the object of the action.

We want to emphasize the fact that students are receiving the diplomas. We want to de-emphasize the fact that the university officials are the people responsible for handing out the diplomas.

> Example: Diplomas *are handed out* on graduation day every year.

The passive can also take more complicated forms.

> Example: Ronald Reagan was the only former actor *to have been elected* President in the twentieth century.

The general populace of the United States elects the president. We want to emphasize who was elected, rather than who did the electing, so we need to use the perfect form of the passive in the preceding sentence.

Source, Reference, and Citation Guide

Sources

You will need to know about citation and referencing during your time at college, and your exam may have one or two questions in this area.

<u>Primary sources</u> – original information in the form of a text, document, manuscript, survey, or statistical data.

Examples: Archives at the county court house on births and deaths

Records held by an institution

A literary manuscript produced by the author

<u>Secondary sources</u> – commentary, discussion, or analysis of the primary source.

Examples: An independent research report analyzing births and deaths in the county

A newspaper article that comments on the records held by the institution

An article in a scholarly journal that discusses the literary manuscript

Use of sources

Be sure that you know how to use lists of references in your own research. You may encounter an exam question on this research technique.

When you are conducting research for a dissertation, term paper, or report, you should pay special attention to the list of references cited at the end of the book or article.

You can read the sources provided in the list of references, and then identify and note down the names of interesting-looking books and articles that the author has cited. You can then read these sources later and cite them in your own research.

Referencing

You should be able to identify what type of source is being referenced when you look at a citation. Note that citations vary in format, depending on what type of material is being used. Study the following citations and notice the slight differences in format for each one.

Books:

Brown, Mark. (2020). *Old towns: A study in urban development.* Pittsburg: Authors' Press.

Notice that only the year is given for a book. Also note that the title is given in italic font. The place and company of publication are provided at the end of a book citation.

Academic or Scholarly Journal:

Tauton, Rachel. (2019). The use of audio in the English classroom. *Pedagogy and Learning, 23*(4), 13-21.

Notice that the volume and issue numbers [*23*(4)] are provided for a scholarly journal. In addition, the page numbers are given at the end of the citation in the following format: 13-21. The name of the journal is given in italics, but the title of the article is not italicized.

Magazines:

Haas, Assan. (2018, May 9). Power in the new millennium. *Popular Technology, 135*, 28-31.

Notice that the date for a magazine citation is in the following format: (2018, May 9). The issue number will be given (*135*), followed by the page numbers (28-31). The name of the magazine is given in italics, but the title of the article is not italicized.

Newspapers:

Gomez, Joaquin. (2015, January 28). The cost to the taxpayer of state energy policies. *The News Today*, pp. 2B, 3A.

The date for a newspaper citation is in the same format as that of a magazine: (2018 May 9). However, the page numbers for a newspaper state the section and page number in this format: pp. 2B, 3A. The name of the newspaper is given in italics, but the title of the article is not italicized.

Online sources:

Papadopoulos, Maria. (2012). Twenty top study tips. *Lists for Busy People.* Retrieved from https://www.alistapart.com/articles/lists

A URL or web address needs to be provided for citations of online materials. The name of the website is given in italics, but the title of the article is not italicized.

CITATION, REFERENCING, AND PLAGIARISM EXERCISES

1. "The way to get started is to quit talking and begin doing." – *Walt Disney*
   Which of the following correctly integrates the quotation?
   A. According to Walt Disney, "The way to get started is to quit talking and begin doing."
   B. According to Walt Disney, "The way I got started was to quit talking and begin doing."
   C. According to Walt Disney, "The way I got things accomplished was by acting and not talking."
   D. Walt Disney was successful because he worked hard by doing things and did not talk too much.

2. Which of the following best describes the term "secondary source"?
   A. physical evidence from the time under study
   B. a document that was written during the time under study
   C. a source that analyzes or discusses information originally published elsewhere
   D. a compendium of knowledge, such as an encyclopedia

3. Anderson, G. (2015, January 7). Neighborhood decline in American cities. *Society Today*, 125(3), 25-32.
   The item above is from a list of references. Which of the following is being cited?
   A. an article from a scholarly journal
   B. a blog
   C. a newspaper article
   D. a magazine article

4. A student is conducting research on possible interpretations of a new federal regulation on carbon emissions from automobiles. Which of the following pieces of information would not be directly relevant to the student's research?
   A. Excerpts of text from the new federal regulation
   B. Graphs and other visual data from reports on the new federal regulation
   C. Statistical evidence of the way in which previous federal regulations on carbon emissions have been prone to misinterpretation
   D. A scholarly article which concludes that many state and local laws have had various possible interpretations

5. Which of the following is a primary source on the effects of climate change in North America?
   A. An article from a scholarly journal that summarizes previous studies on the subject of global climate change
   B. A scientific study that provides evidence of the effects of climate change on North American cities.
   C. A survey of local residents' opinions on new laws that regulate climate change
   D. A detailed analysis of the pollutants emitted from North American factories

6. Which sentence below best describes the term "primary source"?
   A. a document which was written or physical evidence that was created during the time under study
   B. a document which was written about the item under study
   C. an article that analyzes previous research conclusions or findings
   D. an article that explicates existing research conclusions or findings

7. What is the main purpose of reviewing a reading list when conducting research for a term paper or other research project?
   A. to check for plagiarism in the work of others
   B. to assess the veracity of quotations within the article
   C. to identify further sources to use in your research
   D. to determine whether the list of references has been provided in the correct format

8. Smith, C. (2013). *American history in the twenty-first century.* New York: Independent Publishers.
   The item above is from a list of references. Which of the following is being cited?
   A. a newspaper article
   B. a magazine article
   C. an article from a scholarly journal
   D. a book

9. A student is writing a research paper on the impact of a recent change in state law on educators in high schools in his or her state. Which of the following would be the most relevant secondary source for the student's paper?
   A. A textbook on the history of state law affecting educators in high schools
   B. A newspaper article in which a local elementary school teacher complains about recent changes to the law
   C. An article in a periodical in which high school teachers in the state express their opinions on the law change
   D. Discussions with school board members and parents who reside in the area of the local high school

10. "Many of life's failures are people who did not realize how close they were to success when they gave up." – *Thomas A. Edison*
    Which of the following is an example of plagiarism?
    A. Inventor Thomas Edison believed that many people failed because they "did not realize how close they were to success when they gave up."
    B. Thomas Edison said that many people did not realize how close they were to success when they gave up, and for this reason, they were one of many of life's failures.
    C. Thomas Edison claimed that many people were about to succeed when they admitted defeat.
    D. If you believe that "many people did not realize how close they were to success when they gave up," as Thomas Edison once said, then you must continue striving towards your goal.

GRAMMAR REVIEW SET 1

In the next section, five sets are grammar review exercises are provided. If you are proficient at English grammar, you should be able to complete these exercises very quickly.

1. I don't know _____ the promotion or not.
   A. whether got
   B. he got
   C. if he got
   D. that he got

2. Bob is upset because he saw a bad accident that _____ this morning.
   A. was happening
   B. happened
   C. has happening
   D. happen

3. Someone once advised me _____ to California in the summer.
   A. not to go
   B. not going
   C. not go
   D. if I not go

4. _____ in reading popular novels.
   A. I am interesting
   B. Interesting it is
   C. I am interested
   D. It is interesting

5. That device is a machine _____ digital data.
   A. by which encoded
   B. which are encoded
   C. by which are encoded
   D. which encodes

6. _____ her only once since she went away to college.
   A. I have seen
   B. Did I seen
   C. Have I seen
   D. I see

7. The last few months _____ their toll on him.
   A. taken
   B. have taken
   C. made
   D. have made

8. You would have passed your test _____ more.
   A. had you studied
   B. if you studied
   C. you had studied
   D. would you studied

9. That restaurant has dishes that aren't _____ anywhere else.
   A. to be served
   B. serving
   C. served
   D. to serve

10. _____ it, I can't really say if I like skiing.
    A. Never having tried
    B. Never had trying
    C. Never to have tried
    D. Never to try

11. She would have _____ in the accident had she not put on her seat belt.
    A. injury
    B. been injuring
    C. been injured
    D. to be injured

12. To _____ a long story short, I decided not to go to Los Angeles.
    A. take
    B. make
    C. taking
    D. making

13. People _____ about that new video.
    A. constant talk
    B. constant talking
    C. constantly to be talking
    D. are constantly talking

14. He was evicted from his apartment, but what _____ was pay his rent on time.
    A. he should do
    B. should he do
    C. he should have done
    D. he should be doing

15. The professor was telling us not _____ so much time talking.
    A. spending
    B. to be spending
    C. to spending
    D. be spending

GRAMMAR REVIEW EXERCISES – SET 2

1. We don't have any plans for tonight. How about _____ bowling?
   A. to go
   B. we go
   C. going for
   D. going

2. Teachers get tired of students _____ about how much homework they are given.
   A. to complain
   B. complaints

C. to have complained
D. complaining

3. If you want to go for a hamburger, I _____ one too.
A. like to have
B. feel like to have
C. feel like having
D. feel like I have had

4. The new fitness center _____ next week.
A. be opening
B. is being opening
C. will opening
D. is having its opening

5. Janet told me about the surprise party, although she _____ .
A. mightn't have
B. won't have
C. shouldn't have
D. couldn't have

6. I have seen one of Grant Wood's paintings in a museum, but I _____ .
A. from where can't remember
B. where can't remember
C. can't remember from where
D. can't remember where

7. I'm glad you _____ me that you had already completed the report.
A. had told
B. told
C. were telling
D. tell

8. That presentation was far too advanced _____ as an introductory lecture.
A. to be suiting
B. for suiting
C. to be suitable
D. suitably

9. He is _____ his three brothers.
A. taller of
B. the tallest
C. taller than
D. tallest of

10. I really regret _____ harder to increase my savings.
A. not having tried
B. not to try
C. not to tried
D. not to trying

11. He _____ me to repeat something four times yesterday.
A. had asked
B. asked

C. has been asking
D. had been asking

12. We couldn't have completed the project without Ahmed, who _____ a great deal of expertise to the team.
    A. brought
    B. had brought
    C. will have brought
    D. will be bringing

13. Once he _____ that he wasn't going to be able to go to college, he felt a lot better.
    A. accepts
    B. did accept
    C. will accept
    D. had accepted

14. She was upset about not receiving an invitation; we _____ have invited her.
    A. must
    B. may
    C. should
    D. ought

15. Your monetary compensation agreement is in the envelope _____ was forwarded to your attorney.
    A. which
    B. in which
    C. where
    D. in that

GRAMMAR REVIEW EXERCISES – SET 3

1. I expect her _____ out of her parents' house now that she has finished college.
   A. to move
   B. moving
   C. being moved
   D. to have been moving

2. This isn't my first draft of the assignment; I _____ it.
   A. had yet re-written
   B. re-wrote already
   C. have already re-written
   D. re-written already

3. He's getting married tomorrow, and _____ him so worried.
   A. never have I seen
   B. never I saw
   C. I have seen never
   D. I saw never

4. Perhaps she _____ stay home than go shopping with us.
   A. might better
   B. would rather
   C. much better
   D. could rather

5. He gets _____ grades of all the students in his class.
   A. the best
   B. the better
   C. the best of
   D. better than

6. Just after we _____ , he decided to leave.
   A. had arrived
   B. have arrived
   C. are arriving
   D. were arrived

7. The teacher told me off _____ to class.
   A. to be late
   B. to being late
   C. for being late
   D. being late

8. I'm sure that _____ to Disneyland will be a lot of fun.
   A. to go
   B. going
   C. to be going
   D. having gone

9. In addition to _____ , Susan also does knitting.
   A. sew
   B. she sews
   C. sewing
   D. she sewing

10. My new job is going well now that I have gotten used _____ so early.
    A. to getting up
    B. getting up
    C. to get up
    D. get up

11. _____ my best friend only once since she moved to Minneapolis.
    A. I have seen
    B. Did I see
    C. Have I seen
    D. I saw

12. The doctor advised me to do something that I never would have thought _____.
    A. to be done
    B. to do
    C. to doing
    D. of doing

13. It was time John _____ the situation.
    A. accept
    B. accepted
    C. accepts
    D. was accepting

14. The new supermarket is believed _____ next week.
    A. be closing
    B. to be closing
    C. it is closing
    D. to having its closing

15. That problem is between you and _____; you shouldn't discuss it with anyone else.
    A. I
    B. me
    C. mine
    D. my

GRAMMAR REVIEW EXERCISES – SET 4

1. I have no idea where I put my jacket. It could be _____.
   A. anywhere
   B. elsewhere
   C. somewhere else
   D. other place

2. The remodeling on the upstairs of our house is _____ finished.
   A. soon
   B. almost
   C. near
   D. far

3. Although he was extremely careful driving the car, he _____ an accident.
   A. did
   B. has
   C. do have
   D. did have

4. You can put that bag on the seat between you and _____.
   A. I
   B. me
   C. mine
   D. my

5. Many people like going for long walks in the park, but _____ do not.
   A. another
   B. other
   C. others
   D. some other

6. That new student, _____ remember, is supposed to be very intelligent.
   A. whose name I can't
   B. which name I can't
   C. that I can't name
   D. whom I can't name

7. There were many casualties in the area, even though the weather report said that _____ prepared for the tornado.
   A. people should
   B. people should have

      C. people ought have
      D. ought people have

8. At 6'4" Jane is the _____ four sisters.
      A. tallest of the
      B. taller of her
      C. taller than her
      D. most tall of the

9. Sarah told everyone my secret, but _____ we are still good friends.
      A. furthermore
      B. despite of that
      C. contrarily
      D. in spite of that

10. I would have bought that new dress _____ more money.
      A. did I have
      B. have I have
      C. if I did have
      D. had I had

11. I finally decided _____ New College after I got confirmation of my scholarship.
      A. to attend
      B. to attend to
      C. attending
      D. to attend at

12. He got _____ cheating on the exam.
      A. down with
      B. through with
      C. away with
      D. up to

13. We arrived at a solution that can _____ .
      A. be achieved easy
      B. be easily achieved
      C. easy to be achieved
      D. easily to be achieved

14. He is so shy that not a word _____ during the meeting yesterday.
      A. he did say
      B. was he saying
      C. did he say
      D. was it said

15. Our business is going quite well now that we have acquired all _____ we need to sell.
      A. to the merchandise
      B. of the merchandise
      C. for the merchandise
      D. of merchandise

16. After the fire last week, the all of the paintings in the museum are believed _____ .
      A. to have been destroyed
      B. destroying

C. that are destroyed
D. to destroy

17. My grandma is coming to visit me _____ the beginning of the month.
    A. in
    B. at
    C. on
    D within

18. If you hadn't eaten so much, you _____ a stomach ache.
    A. might not have gotten
    B. ought not to have gotten
    C. might have gotten
    D. could get

19. _____ book is the best one I've read so far.
    A. Those
    B. This
    C. Their's
    D. These

20. You're a fool if you believe her because she has told those lies and many _____ .
    A. other
    B. another
    C. others
    D. anothers

GRAMMAR REVIEW EXERCISES – SET 5

1. She is such a nervous person that very rarely _____ relaxed.
   A. she appears
   B. she is appearing
   C. does she appear
   D. she does appear

2. The paper is in the cabinet _____ we use to store the pens and pencils.
   A. that
   B. there
   C. where
   D. in which

3. Starting a new business involves sizing _____ the competition.
   A. around
   B. under
   C. up
   D. over

4. We hope _____ on vacation on Saturday.
   A. to go
   B. to going
   C. going
   D. to have been going

5. No sooner _____ at the party than Sung Li came in.
   A. we arrived
   B. we had arrived
   C. had we arrived
   D. we were arriving

6. Alison is at home recovering _____ the flu.
   A. with
   B. to
   C. for
   D. from

7. She wouldn't have gotten fired _____ honest.
   A. she was
   B. had she been
   C. was she
   D. she had been

8. That was a pretty good movie, but I prefer the one _____ .
   A. to which I saw last week
   B. I saw last week
   C. which last week I saw
   D. I saw it last week

9. I requested that my friend _____ to the party.
   A. to be invited
   B. be inviting
   C. to have been invited
   D. be invited

10. Iced tea on a hot summer day is one of life's _____ pleasures.
    A. greater
    B. most great
    C. greatest
    D. the greatest

11. That form was compulsory, so _____ it in.
    A. you should have filled
    B. should you have filled
    C. should have you filled
    D. you should filled

12. I don't want to eat at McDonalds. I would rather eat _____ .
    A. anyplace
    B. somewhere else
    C. somewhere
    D. other place

13. _____ students here study a lot and work hard.
    A. Almost
    B. Most of
    C. Almost of
    D. Most

14. The suspects were interrogated, but all of them denied _____ the car.
    A. stealing
    B. to steal
    C. to stealing
    D. to have stolen

15. Although some people can't stand our boss, I can put _____ her sometimes.
    A. down
    B. in for
    C. up with
    D. off

16. _____ my exam today, I wanted to get a good night's sleep last night.
    A. While I have
    B. Because of
    C. While having
    D. Because having

17. She has many _____ hobbies apart from fitness and hiking.
    A. other
    B. another
    C. others
    D. more of

18. I know you are normally very careful, but you _____ to be extra cautious when you travel.
    A. did need
    B. do need
    C. have needed
    D. did

19. Although I will leave this job tomorrow, I feel so happy _____ with such wonderful people.
    A. to have
    B. to have worked
    C. to have been worked
    D. worked

20. Even though the three of you have argued, _____ shouldn't have hard feelings against her.
    A. you and he
    B. you and him
    C. him and you
    D. yours and his

SENTENCE CORRECTION AND REVISION PRACTICE SET 1

Select the best substitute for the underlined parts of the following ten sentences. The first answer [choice A] is identical to the original sentence. If you think the original sentence is best, then choose A as your answer.

1. Although only sixteen years old, <u>the university accepted her application because of her outstanding grades</u>.
   A. the university accepted her application because of her outstanding grades.
   B. her application was accepted by the university because of her outstanding grades.
   C. her outstanding grades resulted in her application being accepted by the university.
   D. she was accepted to study at the university because of her outstanding grades.

2. Never in my life <u>have I seen such a beautiful sight.</u>
   A. have I seen such a beautiful sight.
   B. I have seen such a beautiful sight
   C. such a beautiful sight I have seen.
   D. such a beautiful sight I saw.

3. After the loss of a loved one, the bereaved can experience <u>shock, numbness, and they also get depressed.</u>
   A. shock, numbness, and they also get depressed.
   B. shock, numbness, and depression.
   C. shock, numbness, and get depressed.
   D. shock, numbness, and depressed.

4. I was going to study this <u>evening, however the noise next door</u> made it impossible.
   A. evening, however the noise next door
   B. evening: however the noise next door
   C. evening, however, the noise next door
   D. evening. However, the noise next door

5. She was hoping to buy <u>a new car which would be spacious enough to transport</u> her equipment.
   A. a new car which would be spacious enough to transport
   B. a new car, which would be spacious enough to transport
   C. a new car – which would be spacious enough to transport
   D. a new car, that would be spacious enough to transport

6. Near a small <u>river, at the bottom of the canyon we discovered a cave.</u>
   A. river, at the bottom of the canyon we discovered a cave.
   B. river at the bottom of the canyon we discovered a cave.
   C. river at the bottom of the canyon, we discovered a cave.
   D. river, at the bottom of the canyon, we discovered, a cave.

7. <u>Who did the interview panel select</u> for the job?
   A. Who did the interview panel select
   B. Whom did the interview panel select
   C. Who the interview panel selected
   D. Whom the interview panel selected

8. They played <u>the song "Always and Forever"</u> at their wedding reception.
   A. the song "Always and Forever"
   B. the song, "Always and Forever,"

      C.   the song "Always and Forever,"
      D.   the song "Always and Forever",

9. He lost his <u>scholarship, as a consequence of his poor grades.</u>
    A.   scholarship, as a consequence of his poor grades.
    B.   scholarship as a consequence of his poor grades.
    C.   scholarship, as a consequence his poor grades.
    D.   scholarship, as a consequence of, his poor grades.

10. <u>If I was a millionaire, I would give</u> money to charity.
    A.   If I was a millionaire, I would give
    B.   If I was a millionaire, I will give
    C.   If I were a millionaire, I would give
    D.   If I were a millionaire, I will give

Rewrite the following ten sentences mentally in your own head. Follow the directions given for the formation of the new sentence. Remember that your new sentence should be grammatically correct and convey the same meaning as the original sentence.

11. *She worked all night, but she still did not finish the project.*
Rewrite, beginning with: <u>Even though</u>
The next words will be:
    A.   she working all night
    B.   she worked all night
    C.   working all night
    D.   worked all night

12. *While snow showers are common in the north during the winter, precipitation is unlikely tomorrow.*
Rewrite, beginning with: <u>Despite</u>
The next words will be:
    A.   snow showers are common
    B.   of snow showers being common
    C.   snow showers being common
    D.   snow showers as common

13. *Warm all year round, Florida has many out-of-state visitors during December and January.*
Rewrite, beginning with: <u>Because</u>
The next words will be:
    A.   warm all year round,
    B.   of warm all year round,
    C.   of all-year-round warm,
    D.   it is warm all year round,

14. *Tom is highly intelligent, and so is his younger brother.*
Rewrite, beginning with: <u>Just as</u>
Your new sentence will include:
    A.   so too is his younger brother
    B.   as well as his younger brother
    C.   in the same way, his younger brother
    D.   his younger brother, similarly

15. *Mary arrived at the party. Then I decided to go home.*
    Rewrite, beginning with: <u>After</u>
    The next words will be:
    A. Mary arriving at the party
    B. Mary had arrived at the party
    C. arriving at the party
    D. arrived at the party

16. *You will succeed at college if you work hard.*
    Rewrite, beginning with: <u>Provided</u>
    The next words will be:
    A. hard work
    B. work hard
    C. you work hard
    D. that your work hard

17. *She is a good teacher because she is kind and patient.*
    Rewrite, beginning with: <u>Kind and patient</u>
    Your new sentence will include:
    A. of a good teacher
    B. is a good teacher
    C. make a good teacher
    D. which a good teacher

18. *Apart from being rude, she is also stingy.*
    Rewrite, beginning with: <u>Besides</u>
    The next words will be:
    A. being rude
    B. of being rude
    C. of rudeness
    D. she is rude

19. *The teacher became upset because the student was insolent.*
    Rewrite, beginning with: <u>Because of</u>
    The next words will be:
    A. being upset
    B. the teacher was upset
    C. the student was insolent
    D. the student's insolence

20. *More and more teenagers are developing type II diabetes.*
    Rewrite, beginning with: <u>Increasing</u>
    The next words will be:
    A. teenagers
    B. teenage diabetes
    C. numbers of teenagers
    D. amount of teenagers

SENTENCE CORRECTION AND REVISION PRACTICE SET 2

Instructions: Select the best substitute for the underlined parts of the following ten sentences. The first answer [choice A] is identical to the original sentence. If you think the original sentence is best, then choose A as your answer.

1. The child tried to grab the cookies from the <u>shelf, however they were</u> out of reach.
   A. shelf, however they were
   B. shelf: however they were
   C. shelf. However, they were
   D. shelf however, they were

2. Covered in chocolate <u>frosting, the hostess dropped the cake</u> in front of all her guests.
   A. frosting, the hostess dropped the cake
   B. frosting, the hostess cake dropped
   C. frosting, the cake was dropped by the hostess
   D. frosting, by the hostess the cake was dropped

3. <u>To love and be loved</u> is the greatest happiness of existence.
   A. To love and be loved
   B. Loving and be loved
   C. Loving and to be loved
   D. To love and being loved

4. He wanted to buy a <u>telescope, one which he could</u> use to gaze at the stars.
   A. telescope, one which he could
   B. telescope, which one he could
   C. telescope one which he could
   D. telescope. One which he could

5. No sooner <u>I had finished gardening than</u> it began to rain.
   A. I had finished the gardening than
   B. I finished the gardening than
   C. had I finished the gardening than
   D. had finished I the gardening than

6. If <u>I went out</u> alone after dark, I try to be more alert and careful.
   A. I went out
   B. I go out
   C. I had gone out
   D. I were going out

7. "I am not really interested in <u>this movie" he</u> said.
   A. this movie" he
   B. this movie," he
   C. this movie" . he
   D. this movie." He

8. <u>When a person is confused about his or her identity, this</u> is known as an identity crisis.
   A. When a person is confused about his or her identity, this
   B. When you are confused about your identity, this
   C. The experience of confusion about one's own identity, this
   D. The experience of confusion about one's own identity

9. <u>Upset, from receiving the bad news, Mary</u> broke down and cried.
   A. Upset, from receiving the bad news, Mary
   B. Upset, from receiving the bad news Mary
   C. Upset from receiving the bad news, Mary
   D. Upset from receiving the bad news Mary,

10. <u>Dilapidated and disheveled the house appeared</u> forlorn and abandoned.
    A. Dilapidated and disheveled the house appeared
    B. Dilapidated and disheveled the house, appeared
    C. Dilapidated and disheveled the house appeared,
    D. Dilapidated and disheveled, the house appeared

Rewrite the following ten sentences mentally in your own head. Follow the directions given for the formation of the new sentence. Remember that your new sentence should be grammatically correct and convey the same meaning as the original sentence.

11. She wanted that new car for so long, and when she finally got it, she was so excited. Rewrite, beginning with: <u>She was excited because she</u>
    Your new sentence will include:
    A. wanting that new car
    B. that new car, which
    C. that new car which
    D. which she finally got

12. It will be easy to pass my math test, but I cannot say the same about my physics test. Rewrite, beginning with: <u>Unlike my physics test,</u>
    The next words will be:
    A. it will be easy
    B. I should easily
    C. my math test
    D. passing math

13. She felt ill for days and eventually came down with the flu.
    Rewrite, beginning with: <u>Having felt</u>
    Your new sentence will include:
    A. daily illness
    B. eventually down she came
    C. the flu eventually came
    D. she eventually came down

14. If she could afford it, she would come to Hawaii with us.
    Rewrite, beginning with: <u>She is not able to come to Hawaii with us</u>
    The next words will be:
    A. because she
    B. without her
    C. although there
    D. without enough

15. The referee blew his whistle, and then the game began.
    Rewrite, beginning with: <u>The game began</u>
    The next words will be:
    A. the referee blowing
    B. and the referee

C. after the referee
D. although the referee

16. Thomas studied extensively for his final exams, but Mary did not do likewise.
    Rewrite, beginning with: Whereas Thomas
    Your new sentence will include:
    A. unlike Mary
    B. Mary did not
    C. Mary did too
    D. so did Mary

17. He will only get the promotion if he receives approval from his superiors.
    Rewrite, beginning with: Unless he receives approval from his superiors,
    The next words will be:
    A. the promotion will be
    B. he will be
    C. he will get
    D. he will not get

18. In spite of giving her best effort, Barbara failed to complete the project on time. Rewrite, beginning with: Although
    The next words will be:
    A. she gave
    B. her effort
    C. her giving
    D. she failed completing

19. Sarah's father was a foreign diplomat, so she has lived in many locations around the world
    Rewrite, beginning with: Sarah, whose
    Your new sentence will include:
    A. because she has lived
    B. because her father was
    C. she has lived in
    D. has lived in

20. Famous for its high academic standards, Harvard attracts the best and brightest students each year.
    Rewrite, beginning with: Because of
    The next words will be:
    A. the best and the brightest
    B. its high academic standards
    C. attracting the best
    D. famous for its

SENTENCE CORRECTION AND REVISION PRACTICE SET 3

Instructions: Select the best substitute for the underlined parts of the following ten sentences. The first answer [choice A] is identical to the original sentence. If you think the original sentence is best, then choose A as your answer.

1. While at the mall, <u>a paperback book was purchased by me.</u>
   - A. a paperback book was purchased by me.
   - B. the paperback book was purchased by me.
   - C. a paperback book's purchase was made by me.
   - D. I purchased a paperback book.

2. <u>We just arrived</u> at the airport when Tom's flight landed.
   - A. We just arrived
   - B. Just had we arrived
   - C. We had just arrived
   - D. Just we were arriving

3. We were going to go away on <u>vacation. And then</u> our plans changed.
   - A. Vacation. And then
   - B. vacation, then
   - C. vacation and then
   - D. vacation, and then

4. John's favorite hobbies are <u>to read and to swim.</u>
   - A. to read and to swim.
   - B. to read and swimming.
   - C. reading and swimming.
   - D. reading and to swim.

5. <u>Exasperated, Bill finally lost his temper</u> with his unruly children.
   - A. Exasperated, Bill finally lost his temper
   - B. Bill was exasperated, finally lost his temper
   - C. Bill, was exasperated, finally lost his temper
   - D. Exasperating Bill, finally lost

6. He was planning on finding a new <u>apartment that</u> would accommodate all of his oversized furniture.
   - A. apartment that
   - B. apartment. One that
   - C. apartment, that
   - D. apartment so that

7. "I can't believe you won the <u>lottery", Sarah</u> exclaimed.
   - A. lottery", Sarah
   - B. lottery." Sarah
   - C. lottery!" Sarah
   - D. lottery" Sarah

8. <u>In spite of he studied hard, he</u> failed the exam.
   - A. In spite of he studied hard, he
   - B. In spite of studying hard, he
   - C. In spite of he studying hard, he
   - D. In spite of studied hard, he

9. Zanab is the <u>smarter of</u> the three sisters.
   A. smarter of
   B. smarter than
   C. most smart of
   D. smartest of

10. <u>If stealing money from your employer,</u> you could be charged with the crime of embezzlement.
    A. If stealing money from your employer,
    B. Stealing money from your employer
    C. If you steal money from your employer,
    D. If you steal money from your employer

Rewrite the following ten sentences mentally in your own head. Follow the directions given for the formation of the new sentence. Remember that your new sentence should be grammatically correct and convey the same meaning as the original sentence.

11. After checking the extent of the man's injuries, the paramedics put him into the ambulance.
    Rewrite, beginning with: <u>Once they</u>
    The next words will be:
    A. were checking
    B. had checked
    C. had been checking
    D. will check

12. The professor's praise of my exam score in front of the other students embarrassed me. Rewrite, beginning with: <u>I was embarrassed when</u>
    The next words will be:
    A. the professor praised
    B. the professor praising
    C. the professor, praising
    D. the professor, he praised

13. Both Minnesota and Wisconsin get extremely cold in the winter.
    Rewrite, beginning with: <u>Like Minnesota,</u>
    The next words will be:
    A. Wisconsin gets
    B. and Wisconsin
    C. extreme cold
    D. it is

14. Rich in natural beauty and abundant in wildlife, the Grand Canyon is a popular tourist destination.
    Rewrite, beginning with: <u>The Grand Canyon</u>
    Your new sentence will include:
    A. because being
    B. because it being
    C. because it is
    D. because being it

15. My sister was ill, so she stayed home from school.
    Rewrite, beginning with: <u>My sister,</u>
    The next words will be:
    A. ill and
    B. she was ill

C. was ill
D. who was ill

16. If it rains tomorrow, we will have to cancel the picnic.
    Rewrite, beginning with: In the event of
    The next words will be:
    A. raining
    B. rains
    C. rain
    D. it rains

17. The team lost the championship game, and the players were so disappointed.
    Rewrite, beginning with: The team was
    Your new sentence will include:
    A. although it lost
    B. when it lost
    C. and it lost
    D. because the loss of

18. Despite years of training, he was not selected for the Olympics.
    Rewrite, beginning with: Although
    The next words will be:
    A. he trained for years
    B. training for years
    C. years of training
    D. years he trained

19. As he watched television, he fell asleep and began snoring.
    Rewrite, beginning with: Watching
    The next words will be:
    A. television he fell
    B. and fell
    C. television, he fell
    D. television, and falling

20. Many students suffer from homesickness during their studies at colleges in other states.
    Rewrite, beginning with: Suffering from
    Your new sentence will include:
    A. common student's
    B. is common studying
    C. is commonality of students
    D. is common among students

SENTENCE CORRECTION AND REVISION PRACTICE SET 4

Each of the sentences below has four underlined parts. Read each sentence and determine whether any of the underlined parts contains an error in grammar or use. If so, select the underlined part that contains the error as your answer. If the sentence contains no error, then select "No error." No sentence contains more than one error.

1. One of the first skyscrapers to be erected in New York, at the site where its television mast would be most effective, the Empire State Building was constructed in the Art Deco style around 1930. No error

2. Even though chicory is usually cooked, their leaves can be eaten in various ways, including as a raw ingredient in salads or as a dried and ground substitute for coffee. No error

3. Many composers promote nationalism in their work, but what is different about Mussorgsky's compositions are the overt patriotism in his operas. No error

4. Lymph glands, masses of tissue that form part of the lymphatic system, filter bacteria and organisms from organ's in the body and allow lymph to flow into capillaries and from them into lymph vessels. No error

5. Scientifically speaking , almost any positive electric charge can produce a unit of energy from which a volt of electricity is derived. No error

6. It is difficult to know when people first began to grow sweet potatoes because early settlers often did not differentiate this vegetable to other tubers. No error

7. Although companies try to price their products competitively, they often cannot , in spite of their best plans, introduce no new merchandise into the market at a profit. No error

8. Commencing in 1847 and for nearly 16 years thereafter, Mexico City was occupied by U.S. troops until it was conquered by Maximilian, a ruler whose name originates from the roman word *maximus*. No error

9. Ratified at the end of 1992 , the North American Free Trade Agreement eliminated trade barriers among Canada and the United States in order to increase trade and to enable each of the counties to find its unique market position. No error

10. Scientists have discovered that most comets in orbit around the sun , seem to be composed of rock and dust particles embedded in ice. No error

11. Since Christopher Columbus believed that he had established a route between the East Indies and China, subsequent explorer's journeys were impeded by all other theories requiring them to think otherwise. No error

12. Some residents of the former East Germany opposed the dismantling of the Berlin Wall, while others despaired of its very existence because many residents die when attempting to cross it. No error

13. Originally focusing on suffrage, the Women's Rights Movement expanded to include much more than the right to vote and effected the role of women in many countries around the world. No error

14. The Inca migration from the Peruvian highlands to the area west of the Andes constitute an example of the consolidation and extension of the tribe's empire in South America. No error

15. When a government establishes a public sector borrowing requirement, it raises money through the issuance of stocks and bonds, which not only increases its available funds and also forms part of the national debt. No error

16. Ceded by the British to the United States in 1783, the Territory of Wisconsin was inhabited by settlers who differed from that of other territories, not settling the region in haste as newcomers to other states did. No error

17. Born in Hamlet , North Carolina, John Coltrane was arguably one of the most famous of all jazz musicians having played the saxophone. No error

18. A rope and pulley system, an everyday apparatus that easily lifts heavy items, having long been recognized by physicists as a useful application of applied force. No error

19. Great Danes, large hunting dogs that were bred originally by Germans, were once the principle companion animal for the wealthy. No error

*Select the best substitute for the **highlighted** parts of the following ten sentences. The first answer [choice A] is identical to the original sentence. If you think the original sentence is best, then choose A as your answer.*

20. The name "catfish" is applied to a very large family of freshwater fish called the Siluriformes, which have whisker-like barbels **growing from its mouth**.
    A. growing from its mouth.
    B. growing from it's mouth.
    C. growing from their mouths.
    D. grown from the mouth.
    E. to grow from the mouth.

21. While driving the car this afternoon, **the tire suddenly went flat and I was surprised.**
    A. the tire suddenly went flat and I was surprised.
    B. the tire suddenly went flat, and I was surprised.
    C. I was surprised when the tire suddenly went flat.
    D. it was a surprise when the tire suddenly went flat.
    E. it was a surprise as the tire suddenly went flat.

22. Best known for his science fiction classic *Star Wars*, US film producer and director George Lucas was revolutionary at the time for having worked with Francis Ford Coppola, retaining the merchandising rights for his works, **and the special effects to be used in his movies.**
    A. and the special effects to be used in his movies.
    B. and using special effects in his movies.
    C. and the special effects used in his movies.
    D. and the special effects he used in his movies.
    E. and used special effects in his movies.

23. We were planning a picnic for the kids in the park **this afternoon, the rain made it impossible.**
    A. this afternoon, the rain made it impossible.
    B. this afternoon, the rain making it impossible.
    C. this afternoon, with the rain made it impossible.
    D. this afternoon, but the rain made it impossible.
    E. this afternoon, it was the rain that made it impossible.

24. It is said that Roosevelt's favorite pursuits were **to read, play games, and doing crossword puzzles.**
    A. to read, play games, and doing crossword puzzles.
    B. to read, games, and crossword puzzles.
    C. reading, gaming and do crossword puzzles.
    D. reading, games, and doing crossword puzzles
    E. reading, playing games, and doing crossword puzzles.

25. **Being frustrated and fed up, and tired from a hard week at work,** she decided it was time to go away on vacation.
    A. Being frustrated and fed up, and tired from a hard week at work,
    B. Being frustrated and fed up, and she was tired from a hard week at work,
    C. With being frustrated and fed up, and tired from a hard week at work,
    D. Frustrated, fed up, and tired from a hard week at work,
    E. Frustrated and fed up, and also tired from a hard week at work,

26. With his unconventional style, E.E. Cummings inspired a generation of experimental artists called "avant-garde poets," **who disregarded poetic form and rebelling** against the use of traditional spelling and punctuation in verse.
    A. who disregarded poetic form and rebelling
    B. who disregarding poetic form and rebelling
    C. who disregarded poetic form and rebelled
    D. to disregard poetic form and rebelling
    E. who, disregarding poetic form to rebel

27. An outstanding military commander and statesman, George Washington **having strictly avoided** overstepping the constitutional limitations of presidential power.
    A. having strictly avoided
    B. having to strictly avoid
    C. has strictly avoided
    D. was strictly avoiding
    E. strictly avoided

28. Dolomite, otherwise known as calcium-magnesium carbonate, is one of many minerals in **sedimentary rock forming crystals** and to be used for ornamental purposes.
    A. sedimentary rock forming crystals
    B. sedimentary rock formations of crystals
    C. sedimentary rock to form crystals
    D. sedimentary rock having formed crystals
    E. sedimentary rock that had formed crystals

29. **Despite the fact he worked overtime several days in a row the congressman** didn't finish his report on time.
    A. Despite the fact he worked overtime several days in a row the congressman
    B. Despite the fact that he worked overtime several days in a row, the congressman
    C. In spite of the fact working overtime several days in a row, the congressman
    D. Although overtime was worked several days in a row, the congressman
    E. He worked overtime several days in a row, however the congressman

30. **If text messaging while at the wheel** you could be charged with dangerous driving in some states.
    A. If text messaging while at the wheel
    B. While text messaging at the wheel,
    C. If you text message while at the wheel,

D. If you text messaging while at the wheel,
E. Text messaging at the wheel

SENTENCE CORRECTION AND REVISION PRACTICE SET 5

Instructions for Questions 1 to 19 – Each of the sentences below has four underlined parts. Read each sentence and determine whether any of the underlined parts contains an error in grammar or use. If so, select the underlined part that contains the error as your answer. If the sentence contains no error, then select "No error." No sentence contains more than one error.

1. Geologists have noted that petroleum is a chemical compound consisting of a complex mixture of hydrocarbons , that appear to be formed from the bodies of long-dead organisms. No error

2. Magnetism occurs when a current is associated with a field of force and with a north-south polarity, which means that any substance tends to align themselves with the field. No error

3. Charlemagne was crowned King of the Franks in 768, and for approximately 46 years afterwards, he engaged in a brutal conquest of Europe, including the campaign against the moorish people in Spain. No error

4. While both the Black Mountain Poets and the Beat Poets shunned social convention through their experimental art forms, the Black Mountain Poets were affiliated with the Black Mountain College in North Carolina, whereas the Beat Poets were concentrated in California. No error

5. Situated at the site where the Pacific Ocean meets the San Francisco Bay, the Golden Gate spanned by its now-famous bridge , which was completed in 1937. No error

6. Although epiphytes are plants which used other plants for support, they are not parasitic because they have broad leaves that catch water as it drips through the canopy of the tropical forest. No error

7. Theoretically _ bacterial meningitis is far more serious than the viral form of the disease, even though viral meningitis, like any viral disease, can result in an infection for which antibiotics will be ineffective. No error

8. He was desperate to improve his grades before graduation ; However, he could not, due to the constant distraction from after-school activities, see any academic progress. No error

9. It is possible to predict when lightening will occur because sparks between clouds and the ground are accompanied by light before they are seen as lightening . No error

10. Because it evaluates a horse's ability to execute defined movements, the equestrian disciplines of showjumping and dressage are set in a confined area with everything required for the events in place. No error

11. By the end of 1930 , the International Astrological Union had assigned boundaries on the celestial sphere and grouped stars into 88 constellations. No error

12. John F. Kennedy was indisputably the most important U.S. president having been assassinated during his brief tenure in the Oval Office. No error

13. DDT, an organic compound formerly used in insecticides, was withdrawn from the market because it was highly toxic and proved to have a long-lasting negative impact with the environment. No error

14. When Alexander Graham Bell <u>invented</u> the acoustic telegraph, little did he know that he would <u>not only</u> be known for his <u>experiments</u> with sound, but also <u>going</u> down in history as the father of the modern telephone. <u>No error</u>

15. Harmonic accompaniment, a sound sequence <u>that make</u> a recognizable pattern, has been <u>understood by</u> musicians as <u>nearly always</u> being <u>subordinate to</u> melody. <u>No error</u>

16. <u>Normally</u> grown <u>in</u> warm climates, many types of melons <u>are cultivated</u> in greenhouses nowadays, even out of <u>their</u> usual growing seasons. <u>No error</u>

17. The Hawaiian king Kamehameha _ who was <u>descended from</u> Kamehameha IV, abandoned the Hawaiian constitution and <u>imparted</u> fewer rights to his subjects, <u>as all</u> royal rulers did. <u>No error</u>

18. <u>With</u> books in print in more than 100 countries, Mark Twain's work has had <u>his</u> share of <u>admirers'</u>, as well as an <u>abundance of</u> critics. <u>No error</u>

19. The longest river in the world, the Nile flows <u>from</u> <u>its</u> headstream to the <u>Mediterranean</u> delta in <u>Northeast</u> Egypt. <u>No error</u>

*Instructions for Questions 20 to 30 – Select the best substitute for the **highlighted** parts of the following ten sentences. The first answer [choice A] is identical to the original sentence. If you think the original sentence is best, then choose A as your answer.*

20. The defining characteristics of colleges formed during the Antebellum Period **included its** solicitation of government support, promotion of educational opportunities, and provision for educational and technical students.
    A. included its
    B. included their
    C. includes its
    D. includes their
    E. including the

21. Franz Kafka was one of a handful of European novelists **overcoming** intense self-doubt and see his work published during his lifetime.
    A. overcoming
    B. having overcome
    C. who had overcome
    D. to have overcome
    E. to overcome

22. Non-tariff barriers threaten free trade and limit a country's commerce by impeding **its ability to export, to invest, and their financial growth.**
    A. its ability to export, to invest, and their financial growth.
    B. their ability to export, to invest, and financial growth.
    C. it's ability to export, to invest, and their financial growth.
    D. its ability to export, to invest, and financial growth.
    E. its ability to export, to invest, and to grow financially.

23. The first woman elected to the U.S. Congress, suffragist and pacifist Jeannette Rankin **was stanchly promoting** women's rights during her career.
    A. was stanchly promoting
    B. was promoting stanchly
    C. staunchly promoted

     D. having staunchly promoted
     E. having to staunchly promote

24. The diplomat **mailed the letter to the embassy containing confidential information.**
     A. mailed the letter to the embassy containing confidential information.
     B. mailed the letter to the embassy, containing confidential information.
     C. mailed, containing confidential information, the letter to the embassy.
     D. mailed the letter containing confidential information to the embassy.
     E. containing confidential information, mailed the letter to the embassy.

25. Providing an alternative to other energy sources, nuclear power addresses concerns about **increasing air pollution, decreasing fossil fuels, and helps to control costs associated with rising inflation.**
     A. increasing air pollution, decreasing fossil fuels, and helps to control costs associated with rising inflation.
     B. increasing air pollution, decreasing fossil fuels, and help to control costs associated with rising inflation.
     C. increasing air pollution, decreasing fossil fuels, and controlling costs associated with rising inflation.
     D. increasing air pollution, decreasing fossil fuels, and associated costs with rising inflation.
     E. increasing air pollution, decreasing fossil fuels, and associating costs with rising inflation.

26. **Drafting the *Declaration of Independence* and serving as Secretary of State,** Thomas Jefferson has a prominent place in US history.
     A. Drafting the *Declaration of Independence* and serving as Secretary of State,
     B. Drafting the *Declaration of Independence*, and he served as Secretary of State,
     C. By drafting the *Declaration of Independence*, and he served as Secretary of State,
     D. Drafting the *Declaration of Independence* and to serve as Secretary of State,
     E. With drafting the *Declaration of Independence*, he served as Secretary of State and,

27. **Honeysuckle is a well-known species of climbing plant native to the northern hemisphere and consequently** often grown for ornamental purposes in patios and gardens.
     A. Honeysuckle is a well-known species of climbing plant native to the northern hemisphere and consequently
     B. Honeysuckle is a well-known species of climbing plant native to the northern hemisphere and thus
     C. Honeysuckle is a well-known species of climbing plant native to the northern hemisphere and furthermore
     D. Since honeysuckle is a well-known species of climbing plant native to the northern hemisphere, it is
     E. Honeysuckle is a well-known species of climbing plant native to the northern hemisphere and because it is

28. **Overworked and underpaid many employees seek** help from their union representatives.
     A. Overworked and underpaid many employees seek
     B. Overworked and underpaid, many employees seek
     C. Overworked and underpaid many employees seek,
     D. Overworked, and underpaid many employees seek
     E. Overworked and underpaid many employees, seek

29. With its sub-zero temperatures and frozen landscape, **hardly no one considers Siberia to be the ideal tourist destination.**
     A. hardly no one considers Siberia to be the ideal tourist destination.
     B. no one hardly considers Siberia to be the ideal tourist destination.

- C. hardly no one considers Siberia as the ideal tourist destination.
- D. no one considers Siberia hardly to be the ideal tourist destination.
- E. Siberia can hardly be considered to be the ideal tourist destination.

30. **When air rises and condenses into precipitation, this phenomenon** is known as a low-pressure system.
    - A. When air rises and condenses into precipitation, this
    - B. When air rises and condenses into precipitation, this phenomenon
    - C. The phenomenon of air rising and condensing into precipitation, this
    - D. The phenomenon of air rising and condensing into precipitation
    - E. When air rises and condenses into precipitation, a phenomenon which

VOCABULARY EXERCISES

For questions 1 to 4, choose the answer that has the most similar meaning to the underlined word.

1. Acquiesce most nearly means:
   A. decide
   B. assimilate
   C. ignore
   D. comply

2. Patent most nearly means:
   A. showy
   B. obscure
   C. visible
   D. permitted

3. Lenient most nearly means:
   A. easy-going
   B. improper
   C. lazy
   D. insolent

4. Propitiate most nearly means:
   A. appease
   B. rain
   C. modify
   D. snow

For questions 5 to 8, choose the word or words that best completes the sentence.

5. Gossiping about others can actually be quite _____ since it can destroy personal reputations.
   A. extensive
   B. benevolent
   C. opprobrious
   D. exciting

6. The house was _____ flames by the time the firefighters arrived.
   A. engulfed in
   B. covered by
   C. ignited with
   D. overcome about

7. He sat by the lake, _____ his problems.
   A. reviewing
   B. contemplating
   C. inspiring
   D. living

8. He was _____ into action after seeing the pictures of the refugees.
   A. treated
   B. fabricated
   C. covered
   D. galvanized

For questions 9 to 12, choose the word that best indicates the meaning of the underlined word.

9. She is really temperamental in the morning.
   A. grumpy
   B. alert
   C. sleepy
   D. energetic

10. The new law will set a(n) precedent.
    A. system
    B. exemplar
    C. regulation
    D. authority

11. She was commended for her actions.
    A. praised
    B. reprimanded
    C. reported
    D. criticized

12. Ostensibly, he is a nice person.
    A. obviously
    B. occasionally
    C. seemingly
    D. rarely

For questions 13 to 16, choose the answer that has the most similar meaning to the underlined word.

13. Advocate most nearly means:
    A. judge
    B. adversary
    C. proponent
    D. arbiter

14. Laud most nearly means:
    A. proclaim
    B. honor
    C. observe
    D. bolster

15. Dubious most nearly means:
    A. unfavorable
    B. undeniable
    C. doubtful
    D. pessimistic

16. Perturb most nearly means:
    A. annoy
    B. fascinate
    C. astound
    D. stimulate

For questions 17 to 19, choose the word that best indicates the meaning of the underlined word.

17. He approaches every task with <u>alacrity</u>.
    A. eagerness
    B. reproach
    C. reluctance
    D. wholesomeness

18. The company has been <u>dormant</u> since 2018.
    A. successful
    B. incorporated
    C. viable
    D. inactive

19. She always has the most <u>ingenious</u> ideas.
    A. benevolent
    B. popular
    C. ridiculous
    D. inventive

For questions 20 to 23, choose the word that best completes the sentence.

20. A(n) _____ gas was being used in order to eliminate the infestation, so we had to leave the building for 24 hours.
    A. invisible
    B. toxic
    C. innocuous
    D. luxurious

21. She was usually _____ about other people's motives and often made cynical comments.
    A. trustworthy
    B. reluctant
    C. skeptical
    D. resisting

22. The judge lessened the sentence for the crime due to _____ circumstances.
    A. extenuating
    B. incriminating
    C. implicating
    D. overcoming

23. No one could understand the _____ instructions.
    A. nefarious
    B. expanded
    C. nebulous
    D. completed

For questions 24 and 25, choose the answer that has the most similar meaning to the underlined word.

24. <u>Servility</u> most nearly means:
    A. hospitality
    B. abandonment
    C. hostility
    D. submissiveness

25. <u>Indispensable</u> most nearly means:
    A. permanent
    B. superfluous
    C. necessary
    D. non-degradable

For questions 26 and 27, choose the answer that has the most similar meaning to the underlined word.

26. <u>Sycophant</u> most nearly means:
    A. musician
    B. flatterer
    C. complainer
    D. superior

27. <u>Upheaval</u> most nearly means:
    A. movement
    B. launch
    C. tumult
    D. hoist

For questions 28 to 31, choose the word that best completes the sentence.

28. The suspect was _____ for the crime.
    A. charged
    B. exonerated
    C. deliberated
    D. relieved

29. Since she often wears vintage and recycled garments, people say that her taste in clothing is very _____.
    A. unconventional
    B. traditional
    C. modern
    D. stingy

30. Their troubled relationship is full of _____.
    A. sarcasm
    B. ambiguity
    C. acrimony
    D. irony

31. Carrying out their complex strategy involved _____ planning.
    A. intricate
    B. manageable
    C. fortuitous
    D. cooperative

For questions 32 to 35, choose the word that best indicates the meaning of the underlined word.

32. The governor decided to show clemency to the prisoners.
    A. justice
    B. peace
    C. mercy
    D. hope

33. He said that we have to abridge the document.
    A. shorten
    B. mail
    C. interpret
    D. file

34. Of all of the volunteers on the campaign, she has been the most stalwart.
    A. dependable
    B. defensive
    C. compromising
    D. resistant

35. The high salary enticed him into accepting the job.
    A. tricked
    B. lured
    C. blackmailed
    D. bribed

For questions 36 to 40, choose the answer that is the best synonym or antonym for the underlined word.

36. Earnest most nearly means the opposite of:
    A. masculine
    B. insincere
    C. athletic
    D. capable

37. Adept most nearly means:
    A. efficient
    B. skilled
    C. awkward
    D. inept

38. Indignant most nearly means:
    A. offended
    B. angry
    C. worried
    D. excited

39. Furor most nearly means:
    A. leader
    B. sorrow
    C. commander
    D. outcry

40. Jovial most nearly means:
    A. supportive
    B. sincere
    C. caring
    D. cheerful

ESSAY SKILLS SECTION

Essay Structure

Most teachers agree that the best essays follow a four or five paragraph format. This format will help to ensure that your essay is well-organized. This format also helps you write longer and more developed essays.

The five-paragraph essay is organized as follows:

Paragraph 1 – This paragraph is the introduction to your essay. It should include a thesis statement that clearly indicates your main idea or overall opinion. It should also give the reader an overview of your supporting or elaborating points. A thesis statement is a sentence that asserts the main idea of your essay.

The best thesis statements are those that contain a central idea that will serve to narrow the focus of the essay and control the flow ideas within it. As such, a thesis statement should not be too general or vague.

A good structure for the thesis statement is to think of it in terms of an assertion plus a reason or explanation. This structure is better than just giving your assertion or opinion on its own because your explanation indicates the direction that your writing is going to take.

You can think of the essay introduction like a funnel: wide at the top and narrow at the bottom. In other words, start off your introduction in a general but interesting way, and then narrow it down to your main idea and specific supporting points. Remember that the introduction announces your main idea and supporting points, while your main body develops them.

Paragraph 2 – The second paragraph is where you elaborate on your first supporting point. It is normally recommended that you state your strongest and most persuasive point in this paragraph.

Paragraph 3 – You should elaborate on your main idea in the third paragraph by providing a second supporting point.

Paragraph 4 – You should mention your third supporting point in the fourth paragraph. This can be the supporting point that you feel to be the weakest.

Paragraph 5 – In the fifth and final paragraph of the essay, you should make your conclusion. The conclusion should reiterate your supporting points and sum up your position.

The four-paragraph essay will follow the same structure as above, with paragraphs 2 and 3 elaborating two key supporting points and paragraph 4 stating the conclusion. If you decide to put four paragraphs in your essay instead of five, each paragraph should be longer and slightly more detailed than that of a five-paragraph essay.

Essay FAQs

What are the different types of essays?

You may be asked to write one of three different types of essay for your exam or as part of your application process.

Generally speaking, these types of essay questions will be in the following categories:

Discursive or expository essays – you will need to explain and discuss a general topic.

Argumentative essays – you will be asked to write about a controversial issue and express your viewpoint on it. Alternatively, the question may ask you to describe the advantages and disadvantages of something.

Personal experience essays – you will be asked to describe a personal situation you faced. You may use the first-person voice with the pronoun "I" in this type of essay.

What is an elaborating idea?

Elaborating ideas include both explanations and examples. Providing clear examples to support your points is extremely important.

Each of your main body paragraphs should contain an example that supports the flow of your writing.

You should elaborate on and explain your examples in order to make your essay easy to follow.

How do elaborating ideas help to raise my essay score?

Elaboration lengthens your essay and gives you more opportunities to demonstrate higher-level grammar, complex sentence construction, and academic vocabulary.

How many elaborating ideas should I have in each paragraph?

This structure roughly equates to two or three elaborating ideas for each body paragraph.

How do I write the conclusion to the essay?

Conclusions can consist of as few as two sentences, provided that the sentences are cohesive, coherent, and well-constructed.

As in other parts of your essay, you will need to reiterate certain concepts in the conclusion, without repeating word for word what you have already written.

Sample Essays:

Look at each essay below. Then identify the thesis statement in each one. Note how each paragraph in the main body gives and elaborating idea and expands upon it. Also study the structure of the introduction and conclusion, as well as the overall structure of each essay itself. Finally, you may wish to make a note of the high-level academic vocabulary used in the essays.

Essay Question 1 – Is it ever socially acceptable to be pleased when others suffer?

Sample Essay 1 – Discursive or Expository Essay:

While feeling pleasure when others suffer is a human emotion to which most of us would not be so quick to admit, there are occasions when it is socially acceptable to take pleasure in the pain of others. Consider, for example, the gratification that the people of European countries would have experienced when Hitler was defeated during the Second World War. Punishment for crime is another occasion where it is not considered untoward to experience satisfaction over the suffering of others. That is to say, although being pleased to see others stricken is normally not acceptable in a civilized society, there are exceptions to this general rule when others have broken the society's norms during times of war or when a criminal is to be punished for his or her wrongdoing.

Unfortunately, in modern times we have all too often seen dictators or other despotic rulers who treat the members of their societies harshly, and in such situations, the reactions of those subjected to these regimes is certainly socially justifiable. Adolph Hitler, arguably the most notorious dictator of the twentieth century, committed countless heinous acts against the inhabitants of several European countries during World War II. Due to his atrocities, previously contented residents of many towns and villages had to flee their homes in fear, leaving behind all of their worldly possessions. The most unfortunate of these persecuted individuals were submitted to unthinkable states of existence in the many death camps that Hitler oversaw. Because they were forced to live in such unimaginable conditions, those that Hitler persecuted must have been gratified when the dictator faced adversity during the war. Once Hitler had encountered the final ultimatum of surrender or death and his regime was overthrown, the relief and satisfaction openly expressed around the world on a personal level was immense.

The notion that the punishment should fit the crime is another instance of the acceptability of taking pleasure in another's suffering. Criminal law, which has been created according to traditional social convention, has been established to ensure that offenders will be justly tried and punished for their crimes. When someone has broken the norms of society in this way, other members of the community feel satisfied because they believe that justice has been served when the offender has been punished. In addition, punishing social wrongs can act as a deterrent to would-be criminals, thereby further reinforcing social norms.

Whereas taking delight in the misfortune of others is a trait that normally would not receive social approbation, the circumstances faced in war and crime fall outside this conventional social restriction. However, it is doubtful that schadenfreude will ever be considered a socially desirable quality outside these two situations.

Essay Question 2 – Most Americans have access to computers and cell phones on a daily basis, making email and text messaging extremely popular. While some people argue that email and texting are now the most convenient forms of personal communication, others believe that electronic communication technology is often used inappropriately. Write an essay for an audience of educated adults in which you take a position on this topic. Be sure to provide reasons and examples to support your viewpoint.

Sample Essay 2 – Argumentative Essay:

There is no disputing the fact that email and SMS technologies have made our lives easier in a variety of ways. Nevertheless, many of us will have had the experience of falling out with a friend or loved one over an email or text message whose content was poorly written or misconstrued. Clearly, there are certain drawbacks to emails and texts since electronic messaging cannot capture the nuances and subtleties of verbal communication. Modern forms of communication such as electronic mail and SMS messaging can cause problems with personal relationships because of three main shortcomings with these media: their impersonal nature, their inability to capture tone and sarcasm, and their easy accessibility at times of anger.

Depending upon the context, the recipient of an email or text message may consider this mode of communication to be insensitive or uncaring. Although email may be practical for conveying straightforward information or facts, electronic messaging would be remarkably inappropriate for events like announcing a death. There is no direct human contact in emails and texts, and during times of loss or tragedy, human warmth and depth of emotion can only truly be conveyed through a phone call, or better still, by talking face to face.

A further problem with emails and texts is that they do not always accurately express the tone which the writer has intended. For instance, it might be possible for the recipient of a sarcastic email message to take its contents literally. The tone of the message may seem abundantly clear to the person who sent it, but sarcastic or ironically humorous utterances can only really be communicated in speech through the tone and inflection of the voice. Without the aid of tone and inflection, certain phrases in an email may come across as demanding, indifferent, or rude.

The danger of having an accessible messaging service readily at hand during times of high emotion is another insidious problem with electronic media. In this day and age, we have heard stories not only of personal break ups that have been conducted by text, but also of employers who fire their staff by email message. Unless the writer of the message has the discipline and self-control to give him- or herself a period of reasoned contemplation before sending the communication, he or she might send a regrettable message that can cause irretrievable damage to a relationship.

While email and texts may therefore be useful for certain aspects of our daily lives, these communication methods need to be handled with care in some situations, particularly when they could be seen as insensitive, when it is possible that the recipient might misinterpret the meaning, or when composed at times of personal agitation or stress. The writer of the message should use judgment and common sense in order to avoid the ill feelings that may be caused to the recipient in these cases.

Essay Question 3 – It is often said that every cloud has a silver lining. Describe a difficult situation that you faced in your personal or professional life and explain how you ultimately worked out the problem to your advantage.

Sample Essay 3 – Personal Experience Essay:

When I received word that my application for college had not been accepted, I thought life as I knew it was going to end. "How could life be so unjust?" I mused, as I saw the upcoming academic year stretch out in front of me like a deserted highway. Little did I know that this delay in my academic path would ultimately lead to something truly wonderful.

If I had realized that a simple administrative error on my part was going to delay my studies, I certainly would have been more careful in submitting the necessary forms. I was so self-assured that I was going to be accepted that I had not even bothered to look for work. Nor had I taken into account where I was going to live. Hence, I embarked upon what could have been a year of self-doubt and recrimination. However, instead of sinking into a quagmire of depression, I decided to take that year as an opportunity to rethink my options. I began to ask myself some hard questions. Did I really want to study in the degree program I had chosen? How committed was I to the idea of financing my own higher education?

I spent weeks scouring the internet for various degree programs and requested a plethora of course catalogues from institutions of higher learning in other states. I then narrowed down my options to nine or ten different colleges.

Invigorated by a new sense of optimism, I requested financial aid and scholarship information from the colleges I had chosen. In the end, three colleges looked the most promising, so I decided to submit applications for admissions, as well as scholarship applications to those places. Then came the really tough part: waiting for a response. Much to my delight, I was accepted for study at a university in California. I was informed that I would receive a decision about my scholarship application within two months.

The joy I felt when I found out that I had received a full scholarship more than outstripped the agony I had experienced less than a year earlier. Had I not had that setback, I never would have decided to pursue a degree in education.

ESSAY CORRECTION EXERCISE 1

The draft essays that follow contain errors. Choose the correct version of each part of each sentence from the answer choices provided. If the part of the sentence is correct as written, you should choose answer A. The answers are provided at the end of the exercises.

[1] Antarctica is a mysterious and remote continent [2] one which is often forgotten by virtue of its geographical location. [3] Now that the Antarctic is remote and desolate. [4] Nevertheless, an understanding of the organisms that inhabit this continent was critical [5] to our comprehension of the world as a global community. [6] For this reason, the southernmost continent has the source of a great deal of scientific investigation.

[7] Many notable recent research has come from America and Great Britain. [8] The British Antarctic Survey, sponsored with the Natural Environment Research Council of the United Kingdom, [9] and the United States Antarctic Resource Center, a collaborate of the United States Geological Survey Mapping Division and the National Science Foundation, [10] are forerunners in the burgeoning currently field of research in this area.

[11] This corpus of research has resulted in an abundance of factual data on the Antarctic. [12] For example, one now know that more than ninety nine percent of the land is completely covered by snow and ice, [13] which making Antarctica the coldest continent on the planet. [14] This inhospitable climate, has not surprisingly, brought about the adaptation [15] of a plethora of plants and biological organisms on the continent present. [16] An investigation for the sedimentary geological formations provides testimony to the process of adaptation. [17] Ancient sediment's recovered from the bottom of Antarctic lakes, [18] bacteria as well as discovered in ice, [19] has reveal the history of climate change over the past 10,000 years.

Item 1.
- A. Antarctica is a mysterious and remote continent
- B. Antarctica is a mysterious and resounding continent
- C. Antarctica is a mysterious and respectable continent
- D. Antarctica is a mysterious and resistant continent
- E. Antarctica is a mysterious and restrained continent

Item 2.
- A. one which is often forgotten by virtue of its geographical location.
- B. one whose often forgotten by virtue of its geographical location.
- C. that is often forgotten by virtue of its geographical location.
- D. this is often forgotten by virtue of its geographical location.
- E. those are often forgotten by virtue of its geographical location.

Item 3.
- A. Now that the Antarctic is remote and desolate.
- B. Always, the Antarctic is remote and desolate.
- C. Since the Antarctic is remote and desolate.

D. Indeed, the Antarctic is remote and desolate.
E. On the other hand, the Antarctic is remote and desolate.

Item 4.
A. Nevertheless, an understanding of the organisms that inhabit this continent was critical
B. Nevertheless, an understanding of the organisms that inhabit this continent were critical
C. Nevertheless, an understanding of the organisms that inhabit this continent is critical
D. Nevertheless, an understanding of the organisms that inhabit this continent are critical
E. Nevertheless, an understanding of the organisms that inhabit this continent are being critical

Item 5.
A. to our comprehension of the world as a global community.
B. to our comprehension at the world as a global community.
C. to our comprehension in the world as a global community.
D. to our comprehension about the world as a global community.
E. to our comprehension for the world as a global community.

Item 6.
A. For this reason, the southernmost continent has the source of a great deal of scientific investigation.
B. For this reason, the southernmost continent has been the source of a great deal of scientific investigation.
C. For this reason, the southernmost continent was the source of a great deal of scientific investigation.
D. For this reason, the southernmost continent has to be the source of a great deal of scientific investigation.
E. For this reason, the southernmost continent had the source of a great deal of scientific investigation.

Item 7.
A. Many notable recent research has come from America and Great Britain.
B. Much notable recent research has come from America and Great Britain.
C. More notable recent research has come from America and Great Britain.
D. More than notable recent research has come from America and Great Britain.
E. As much as notable recent research has come from America and Great Britain.

Item 8.
A. The British Antarctic Survey, sponsored with the Natural Environment Research Council of the United Kingdom,
B. The British Antarctic Survey, sponsored by the Natural Environment Research Council of the United Kingdom,
C. The British Antarctic Survey, sponsored against the Natural Environment Research Council of the United Kingdom,
D. The British Antarctic Survey, sponsored from the Natural Environment Research Council of the United Kingdom,
E. The British Antarctic Survey, sponsored upon the Natural Environment Research Council of the United Kingdom,

Item 9.
A. and the United States Antarctic Resource Center, a collaborate of the United States Geological Survey Mapping Division and the National Science Foundation,
B. And the United States Antarctic Resource Center, a collaborative of the United States Geological Survey Mapping Division and the National Science Foundation,
C. and the United States Antarctic Resource Center, a collaboratively of the United States Geological Survey Mapping Division and the National Science Foundation,

- D. and the United States Antarctic Resource Center, a collaboration of the United States Geological Survey Mapping Division and the National Science Foundation,
- E. and the United States Antarctic Resource Center, a collaborator of the United States Geological Survey Mapping Division and the National Science Foundation,

Item 10.
- A. are forerunners in the burgeoning currently field of research in this area.
- B. are forerunners in the burgeoning field of currently research in this area.
- C. are currently forerunners in the burgeoning field of research in this area.
- D. are forerunners in the burgeoning field of research in currently this area.
- E. are forerunners in the burgeoning field of research in this currently area.

Item 11.
- A. This corpus of research has resulted in an abundance of factual data on the Antarctic.
- B. This corpus of research was resulted in an abundance of factual data on the Antarctic.
- C. This corpus of research has been resulted in an abundance of factual data on the Antarctic.
- D. This corpus of research was resulting in an abundance of factual data on the Antarctic.
- E. This corpus of research resulting in an abundance of factual data on the Antarctic.

Item 12.
- A. For example, one now know that more than ninety nine percent of the land is completely covered by snow and ice,
- B. For example, we now know that more than ninety nine percent of the land is completely covered by snow and ice,
- C. For example, they now knows that more than ninety nine percent of the land is completely covered by snow and ice,
- D. For example, the community now know that more than ninety nine percent of the land is completely covered by snow and ice,
- E. For example, the research now know that more than ninety nine percent of the land is completely covered by snow and ice,

Item 13.
- A. which making Antarctica the coldest continent on the planet.
- B. which is making Antarctica the coldest continent on the planet.
- C. making Antarctica the coldest continent on the planet.
- D. has made Antarctica the coldest continent on the planet.
- E. that made Antarctica the coldest continent on the planet.

Item 14.
- A. This inhospitable climate, has not surprisingly, brought about the adaptation
- B. This inhospitable climate has, not surprisingly, brought about the adaptation
- C. This inhospitable climate has, not surprisingly; brought about the adaptation
- D. This inhospitable climate has not surprisingly: brought about the adaptation
- E. This inhospitable climate has not surprisingly, brought about the adaptation

Item 15.
- A. of a plethora of plants and biological organisms on the continent present.
- B. of a plethora of plants and biological organisms present on the continent.
- C. of a plethora on the continent of plants and biological organisms present.
- D. of a plethora of plants on the continent and biological organisms present.
- E. of a plethora of plants and on the continent biological organisms present.

Item 16.
- A. An investigation for the sedimentary geological formations provides testimony to the process of adaptation.
- B. An investigation within the sedimentary geological formations provides testimony to the process of adaptation.
- C. An investigation at the sedimentary geological formations provides testimony to the process of adaptation.
- D. An investigation about the sedimentary geological formations provides testimony to the process of adaptation.
- E. An investigation into the sedimentary geological formations provides testimony to the process of adaptation.

Item 17.
- A. Ancient sediment's recovered from the bottom of Antarctic lakes,
- B. Ancient sediments' recovered from the bottom of Antarctic lakes,
- C. Ancient sediments recovered from the bottom of Antarctic lakes,
- D. Ancient's sediment recovered from the bottom of Antarctic lakes,
- E. Ancient's sediments recovered from the bottom of Antarctic lakes,

Item 18.
- A. bacteria as well as discovered in ice,
- B. as well as bacteria discovered in ice,
- C. bacteria discovered as well as in ice,
- D. bacteria discovered in as well as ice,
- E. bacteria discovered in ice as well,

Item 19.
- A. has reveal the history of climate change over the past 10,000 years.
- B. has revealed the history of climate change over the past 10,000 years.
- C. have reveal the history of climate change over the past 10,000 years.
- D. have revealed the history of climate change over the past 10,000 years.
- E. have been revealed the history of climate change over the past 10,000 years.

Item 20.
If the student were to add a paragraph at the end of the essay explaining that the reliability of the research on Antarctica has been disputed, the essay would lose:
- A. its academic tone.
- B. its clarity and focus.
- C. the sense that this topic of current interest.
- D. its emphasis on the inhospitality of the Antarctic climate.
- E. the sense of importance it places on the scientific evidence.

ESSAY CORRECTION EXERCISE 2

[1] The major significant characteristic of any population is its age-sex structure, [2] defining as the proportion of people of each gender in each different age group. [3] The age-sex structure determines the potential for reproduction, [4] and for example population growth, [5] based on the balance of males and females of child-bearing age inside a population. [6] Thus, the age-sex structure was social policy implications.

[7] For instance, a population with a high proportion of citizens elderly [8] needs to consider its governmental-funded pension schemes and health care systems carefully. [9] As follows: a demographic with a greater percentage of young children should ensure [10] which its educational funding and child welfare policies are implemented efficaciously. [11] Accordingly, as the composition of a population changes against time, [12] the government may need to restate its funding priorities.

[13] For it is possible that a population may have low birth rates [14] resulting an imbalance in the age-sex structure. [15] Low birth rate's might also be attributable to governmental policy that attempts to control the population. [16] Policies are one example of that restrict the number of children a family can have this outcome.

[17] Other possible reason for these types of demographic changes might be unnaturally high death rates, [18] such like in the case of a disease epidemic or natural disaster. [19] Finally, migration is another factor [20] in demographic attrition, because in any population, a certain amount of people, may decide to emigrate, or move to a different country.

Item 1.
- A. The major significant characteristic of any population is its age-sex structure,
- B. The majorly significant characteristic of any population is its age-sex structure,
- C. The most significantly characteristic of any population is its age-sex structure,
- D. The most significant characteristic of any population is its age-sex structure,
- E. The more significant characteristic of any population is its age-sex structure,

Item 2.
- A. defining as the proportion of people of each gender in each different age group.
- B. defined as the proportion of people of each gender in each different age group.
- C. which defining as the proportion of people of each gender in each different age group.
- D. which defined as the proportion of people of each gender in each different age group.
- E. as defined as the proportion of people of each gender in each different age group.

Item 3.
- A. The age-sex structure determines the potential for reproduction,
- B. The age-sex structure determined the potential for reproduction,
- C. The age-sex structure has determined the potential for reproduction,
- D. The age-sex structure had determined the potential for reproduction,
- E. The age-sex structure was determined the potential for reproduction,

Item 4.
- A. and for example population growth,
- B. and so that population growth,
- C. and with regard to population growth,
- D. and it follows that population growth,
- E. and as a consequence population growth,

Item 5.
- A. based on the balance of males and females of child-bearing age inside a population.
- B. based on the balance of males and females of child-bearing age within a population.
- C. based on the balance of males and females of child-bearing age containing a population.
- D. based on the balance of males and females of child-bearing age consisting a population.
- E. based on the balance of males and females of child-bearing age attributing a population.

Item 6.
- A. Thus, the age-sex structure was social policy implications.
- B. Thus, the age-sex structure is social policy implications.
- C. Thus, the age-sex structure has social policy implications.
- D. Thus, the age-sex structure had social policy implications.
- E. Thus, the age-sex structure does social policy implications.

Item 7.
- A. For instance, a population with a high proportion of citizens elderly
- B. For instance, a population with an elderly high proportion of citizens
- C. For instance, a population with a high proportion elderly of citizens
- D. For instance, a population with a high proportion of elderly citizens
- E. For instance, a population with a high elderly proportion of citizens

Item 8.
- A. needs to consider its governmental-funded pension schemes and health care systems carefully.
- B. needs to consider its governmentally-funded pension schemes and health care systems carefully.
- C. needs to consider its funded-governmental pension schemes and health care systems carefully.
- D. needs to consider its funded-governmentally pension schemes and health care systems carefully.
- E. needs to consider its funded governmentally-pension schemes and health care systems carefully.

Item 9.
- A. As follows: a demographic with a greater percentage of young children should ensure
- B. Just as a demographic with a greater percentage of young children should ensure
- C. Conversely, a demographic with a greater percentage of young children should ensure
- D. Despite, a demographic with a greater percentage of young children should ensure
- E. Unless a demographic with a greater percentage of young children should ensure

Item 10.
- A. which its educational funding and child welfare policies are implemented efficaciously.
- B. that its educational funding and child welfare policies are implemented efficaciously.
- C. which it's educational funding and child welfare policies are implemented efficaciously.
- D. that it's educational funding and child welfare policies are implemented efficaciously.
- E. hence its educational funding and child welfare policies are implemented efficaciously.

Item 11.
- A. Accordingly, as the composition of a population changes against time,
- B. Accordingly, as the composition of a population changes for time,
- C. Accordingly, as the composition of a population changes over time,
- D. Accordingly, as the composition of a population changes past time,
- E. Accordingly, as the composition of a population changes as time,

Item 12.
- A. the government may need to restate its funding priorities.
- B. the government may need to re-evaluate its funding priorities.
- C. the government may need to recuperate its funding priorities.
- D. the government may need to cooperate its funding priorities.
- E. the government may need to instigate its funding priorities.

Item 13.
- A. For it is possible that a population may have low birth rates
- B. For this possible that a population may have low birth rates
- C. This is possible that a population may have low birth rates
- D. It is possible that a population may have low birth rates
- E. That is possible that a population may have low birth rates

Item 14.
- A. resulting an imbalance in the age-sex structure.
- B. because an imbalance in the age-sex structure.
- C. due to an imbalance in the age-sex structure.
- D. since an imbalance in the age-sex structure.
- E. in order to imbalance in the age-sex structure.

Item 15.
- A. Low birth rate's might also be attributable to governmental policy that attempts to control the population.
- B. Low birth's rates might also be attributable to governmental policy that attempts to control the population.
- C. Low births' rates might also be attributable to governmental policy that attempts to control the population.
- D. Low birth rates' might also be attributable to governmental policy that attempts to control the population.
- E. Low birth rates might also be attributable to governmental policy that attempts to control the population.

Item 16.
- A. Policies are one example of that restrict the number of children a family can have this outcome.
- B. Policies that restrict are one example of the number of children a family can have this outcome.
- C. Policies that restrict the number of children a family can have this outcome are one example.
- D. Policies that restrict the number of children a family can have are one example of this outcome.
- E. Policies that restrict the number of children a family are one example of this outcome can have.

Item 17.
- A. Other possible reason for these types of demographic changes might be unnaturally high death rates,
- B. Others possible reason for these types of demographic changes might be unnaturally high death rates,

- C. Another possible reason for these types of demographic changes might be unnaturally high death rates,
- D. Anothers possible reason for these types of demographic changes might be unnaturally high death rates,
- E. Another possible reasons for these types of demographic changes might be unnaturally high death rates,

Item 18.
- A. such like in the case of a disease epidemic or natural disaster.
- B. such as in the case of a disease epidemic or natural disaster.
- C. as such as in the case of a disease epidemic or natural disaster.
- D. as its in the case of a disease epidemic or natural disaster.
- E. as much like as in the case of a disease epidemic or natural disaster.

Item 19.
- A. Finally, migration is another factor
- B. Final migration is another factor
- C. Final, migration is another factor
- D. To end, migration is another factor
- E. Conclusively, migration is another factor

Item 20.
- A. in demographic attrition, because in any population, a certain amount of people, may decide to emigrate, or move to a different country.
- B. in demographic attrition because in any population a certain amount of people may decide to emigrate, or move to a different country.
- C. in demographic attrition because, in any population, a certain amount of people may decide to emigrate or move to a different country.
- D. in demographic attrition because in any population, a certain amount of people may decide to emigrate, or move to a different country.
- E. in demographic attrition because in any population a certain amount of people may decide to emigrate or move to a different country.

Item 21.
Suppose that the student was asked to write an essay, the purpose of which was to explain how the government could rectify current deficiencies in the age-sex structure. Has the student achieved this purpose?
- A. Yes, because the student talks about the government's reassessment of funding priorities.
- B. Yes, because the student describes the social policy implication of the age-sex structure.
- C. Yes, because the student explains the effect of governmental policy on low birth rates.
- D. No, because the student fails to provide sufficient examples of the how governmental policy needs to adapt to population changes over time.
- E. No, because the student does not enumerate specific solutions that the government could attempt.

ESSAY CORRECTION EXERCISE 3

[1] A group of English separatists known as the Pilgrims first left England to live in Amsterdam, in 1608. [2] After spending a few years in their new city, apart from this, many members of the group [3] felt whose they did not have enough independence. [4] Hence, in 1617, the Pilgrims decided to leave Amsterdam immigrating to America.

[5] More of these separatists were poor farmers [6] whom did not have much education or social status, and, not surprisingly, [7] the group had many financial problems that prevented them for beginning their journey. [8] Thereby their inability to finance themselves caused many disputes and disagreements, [9] the Pilgrims finally managing to obtain financing [10] from a well-known and considerable London businessman named Thomas Weston.

[11] Having secured Weston's monetary support, the group returned to England to pick up some additional passengers, [12] and it boarded a large ship called the Mayflower on September 16, 1620. [13] After 65 days at sea, the pilgrim's reached America.

[14] Plymouth a town about 35 miles southeast of Boston in the New England state of Massachusetts [15] was established by the Pilgrims in December 21, 1620. [16] Even though the early days of this new lives were filled with hope and promise, [17] the harsh winter proved being too much for some of the settlers. [18] Near half of the Pilgrims died during that first winter, [19] but those who lived go on to work hard and prosper.

Item 1.
- A. A group of English separatists known as the Pilgrims first left England to live in Amsterdam, in 1608.
- B. A group of English separatists known as the Pilgrims first left England to live, in Amsterdam, in 1608.
- C. A group of English separatists known as the Pilgrims first left England to live in Amsterdam in 1608.
- D. A group of English separatists known as the Pilgrims, first left England to live in Amsterdam, in 1608.
- E. A group of English separatists known as the Pilgrims, first left England to live, in Amsterdam in 1608.

Item 2.
- A. After spending a few years in their new city, apart from this, many members of the group
- B. After spending a few years in their new city, in this case, many members of the group
- C. After spending a few years in their new city, namely, many members of the group
- D. After spending a few years in their new city, however, many members of the group
- E. After spending a few years in their new city, otherwise, many members of the group

Item 3.
- A. felt whose they did not have enough independence.
- B. felt whom they did not have enough independence.
- C. felt which they did not have enough independence.
- D. felt that they did not have enough independence.
- E. felt in that they did not have enough independence.

Item 4.
　A. Hence, in 1617, the Pilgrims decided to leave Amsterdam immigrating to America.
　B. Hence, in 1617, the Pilgrims decided to leave Amsterdam to immigrate to America.
　C. Hence, in 1617, the Pilgrims decided to leave Amsterdam emigrating to America.
　D. Hence, in 1617, the Pilgrims decided to leave Amsterdam to emigrate to America.
　E. Hence, in 1617, the Pilgrims decided to leave Amsterdam for migrating to America.

Item 5.
　A. More of these separatists were poor farmers
　B. Much of these separatists were poor farmers
　C. Many of these separatists were poor farmers
　D. Many more of these separatists were poor farmers
　E. The most of these separatists were poor farmers

Item 6.
　A. whom did not have much education or social status, and, not surprisingly,
　B. of whom did not have much education or social status, and, not surprisingly,
　C. whose did not have much education or social status, and, not surprisingly,
　D. which did not have much education or social status, and, not surprisingly,
　E. who did not have much education or social status, and, not surprisingly,

Item 7.
　A. the group had many financial problems that prevented them for beginning their journey.
　B. the group had many financial problems that prevented them to beginning their journey.
　C. the group had many financial problems that prevented them from beginning their journey.
　D. the group had many financial problems that prevented them against beginning their journey.
　E. the group had many financial problems that prevented them with beginning their journey.

Item 8.
　A. Thereby their inability to finance themselves caused many disputes and disagreements,
　B. Although their inability to finance themselves caused many disputes and disagreements,
　C. Nevertheless their inability to finance themselves caused many disputes and disagreements,
　D. Despite their inability to finance themselves caused many disputes and disagreements,
　E. In spite of their inability to finance themselves caused many disputes and disagreements,

Item 9.
　A. the Pilgrims finally managing to obtain financing
　B. the Pilgrims finally managed obtaining financing
　C. the Pilgrims finally were managed obtaining financing
　D. the Pilgrims finally were managed to obtain financing
　E. the Pilgrims finally managed to obtain financing

Item 10.
　A. from a well-known and considerable London businessman named Thomas Weston.
　B. From a well-known and affluent London businessman named Thomas Weston.
　C. from a well-known and unfortunate London businessman named Thomas Weston.
　D. from a well-known and adamant London businessman named Thomas Weston.
　E. from a well-known and insistent London businessman named Thomas Weston.

Item 11.
　A. Having secured Weston's monetary support, the group returned to England to pick up some additional passengers,
　B. To have secured Weston's monetary support, the group returned to England to pick up some additional passengers,

- C. They have secured Weston's monetary support, the group returned to England to pick up some additional passengers,
- D. When they have secured Weston's monetary support, the group returned to England to pick up some additional passengers,
- E. Having secured Weston's monetary support, the group returned to England to pick up some additional passengers

Item 12.
- A. and it boarded a large ship called the Mayflower on September 16, 1620.
- B. and he or she boarded a large ship called the Mayflower on September 16, 1620.
- C. and one boarded a large ship called the Mayflower on September 16, 1620.
- D. and they boarded a large ship called the Mayflower on September 16, 1620.
- E. and those boarded a large ship called the Mayflower on September 16, 1620.

Item 13.
- A. After 65 days at sea, the pilgrim's reached America.
- B. After 65 days at sea, the Pilgrims' reached America.
- C. After 65 days at sea, the Pilgrims reached America.
- D. After 65 days at sea, Pilgrim's reached America.
- E. After 65 days at sea, Pilgrims' reached America.

Item 14.
- A. Plymouth a town about 35 miles southeast of Boston in the New England state of Massachusetts
- B. Plymouth, a town about 35 miles southeast of Boston in the New England state of Massachusetts,
- C. Plymouth, a town about 35 miles southeast of Boston in the New England, state of Massachusetts
- D. Plymouth, a town about 35 miles southeast of Boston in the New England, state of Massachusetts,
- E. Plymouth, a town about 35 miles southeast of Boston, in the New England, state of Massachusetts,

Item 15.
- A. was established by the Pilgrims in December 21, 1620.
- B. was established by the Pilgrims on December 21, 1620.
- C. was established by the Pilgrims at December 21, 1620.
- D. was established by the Pilgrims upon December 21, 1620.
- E. was established by the Pilgrims during December 21, 1620.

Item 16.
- A. Even though the early days of this new lives were filled with hope and promise,
- B. Even though the early days of that new lives were filled with hope and promise,
- C. Even though the early days of their new lives were filled with hope and promise,
- D. Even though the early days of these new live were filled with hope and promise,
- E. Even though the early days of those new live were filled with hope and promise,

Item 17.
- A. the harsh winter proved being too much for some of the settlers.
- B. the harsh winter proved to be too much for some of the settlers.
- C. the harsh winter proved to being too much for some of the settlers.
- D. the harsh winter proved been too much for some of the settlers.
- E. the harsh winter proved to been too much for some of the settlers.

Item 18.
- A. Near half of the Pilgrims died during that first winter,
- B. Nearly half of the Pilgrims died during that first winter,
- C. Nearly of half of the Pilgrims died during that first winter,
- D. Near of half of the Pilgrims died during that first winter,
- E. Almost near half of the Pilgrims died during that first winter,

Item 19.
- A. but those who lived go on to work hard and prosper.
- B. but those who lived goes on to work hard and prosper.
- C. but those who lived going on to work hard and prosper.
- D. but those who lived went on to work hard and prosper.
- E. but those who lived had went on to work hard and prosper.

Item 20.
If the student removed the last sentence of the essay, how would this affect the essay?
- A. The essay would have more emphasis on the hardships of the Pilgrims.
- B. The comments on the early days of the Pilgrims would have increased importance.
- C. The historical account of the Pilgrims would lack continuity.
- D. The essay would lack a sense of focus.
- E. The essay would lack a proper conclusion.

ESSAY CORRECTION EXERCISE 4

[1] In 1929 that electrical activity in the human brain was first discovered. [2] Hans Berger, the German psychiatrist made the discovery, [3] was despondent to find out, in contrast to, that his research was quickly dismissed by many other scientists.

[4] The work of Berger was confirmed three years later, in 1932, when Edgar Adrian a Briton, [5] clearly demonstrated that the brain, like the heart, is profuse in its electrical activity. [6] Because of Adrian's work, it know that the electrical impulses [7] in the brain called brain waves are a mixture of four different frequencies, [8] that are based on the number of electrical impulses [9] that occurring in the brain per second.

[10] Accordingly, there are four types of brain waves as follows, alpha, beta, delta, and theta. [11] Alpha waves occur in a state of relaxation, while beta waves occur when a person is alert. [12] In addition, delta waves take place for sleep, but they can also occur dysfunctionally when the brain has been severely damaged. [13] Finally, theta waves are a frequency of [14] somewhere in between alpha and delta. [15] Seems that the purpose of theta waves is solely to facilitate the combination of the other brain waves.

[16] The whole notion of brain waves feeds into the current controversy about brain death. [17] Some believe that brain death is characterized by the failure of the cerebral cortex to function. [18] On the other hand, anothers say that mere damage to the cerebral cortex is not enough. [19] They assert that brain stem function must also cease before can a person be declared dead because the cerebral cortex is responsible for other bodily processes.

Item 1.
- A. In 1929 that electrical activity in the human brain was first discovered.
- B. It in 1929 that electrical activity in the human brain was first discovered.
- C. It was in 1929 that electrical activity in the human brain was first discovered.
- D. It in 1929 was that electrical activity in the human brain was first discovered.
- E. That in 1929 electrical activity in the human brain was first discovered.

Item 2.
- A. Hans Berger, the German psychiatrist made the discovery,
- B. Hans Berger, the German psychiatrist had made the discovery,
- C. Hans Berger, the German psychiatrist who made the discovery,
- D. Hans Berger, the German psychiatrist whom made the discovery,
- E. Hans Berger, the German psychiatrist which made the discovery,

Item 3.
- A. was despondent to find out, in contrast to, that his research was quickly dismissed by many other scientists.
- B. was despondent to find out, likewise, that his research was quickly dismissed by many other scientists.
- C. was despondent to find out, but, that his research was quickly dismissed by many other scientists.
- D. was despondent to find out, though, that his research was quickly dismissed by many other scientists.
- E. was despondent to find out, although, that his research was quickly dismissed by many other scientists.

Item 4.
- A. The work of Berger was confirmed three years later, in 1932, when Edgar Adrian a Briton,
- B. The work of Berger was confirmed three years later, in 1932, when Edgar Adrian, a Briton,
- C. The work of Berger was confirmed three years later, in 1932, when Edgar Adrian a Briton
- D. The work of Berger was confirmed three years later, in 1932, when Edgar Adrian a Briton;
- E. The work of Berger was confirmed three years later, in 1932, when Edgar Adrian, a Briton;

Item 5.
- A. clearly demonstrated that the brain, like the heart, is profuse in its electrical activity.
- B. demonstrated that the clearly brain, like the heart, is profuse in its electrical activity.
- C. demonstrated that the brain, like clearly the heart, is profuse in its electrical activity.
- D. demonstrated that the brain, like the heart clearly, is profuse in its electrical activity.
- E. demonstrated that the brain, like the heart, is profuse clearly in its electrical activity.

Item 6.
- A. Because of Adrian's work, it know that the electrical impulses
- B. Because of Adrian's work, it known that the electrical impulses
- C. Because of Adrian's work, it is known that the electrical impulses
- D. Because of Adrian's work, we known that the electrical impulses
- E. Because of Adrian's work, one known that the electrical impulses

Item 7.
- A. in the brain called brain waves are a mixture of four different frequencies,
- B. in the brain, called brain waves are a mixture of four different frequencies,
- C. in the brain called brain waves, are a mixture of four different frequencies,
- D. in the brain, called brain waves, are a mixture of four different frequencies,
- E. in the brain, called brain waves, are a mixture, of four different frequencies,

Item 8.
- A. that are based on the number of electrical impulses
- B. that based on the number of electrical impulses
- C. which are based on the number of electrical impulses
- D. which based on the number of electrical impulses
- E. are based on the number of electrical impulses

Item 9.
- A. that occurring in the brain per second.
- B. that occurred in the brain per second.
- C. that had occurred in the brain per second.
- D. that have occurrence in the brain per second.
- E. that occur in the brain per second.

Item 10.
- A. Accordingly, there are four types of brain waves as follows, alpha, beta, delta, and theta.
- B. Accordingly, there are four types of brain waves as follows: alpha, beta, delta, and theta.
- C. Accordingly, there are four types of brain waves as follows; alpha, beta, delta, and theta.
- D. Accordingly, there are four types of brain waves as follows alpha, beta, delta, and theta.
- E. Accordingly, there are four types of brain waves as follows. Alpha, beta, delta, and theta.

Item 11.
- A. Alpha waves occur in a state of relaxation, while beta waves occur when a person is alert.
- B. Alpha waves occur in a state of relaxation, rather beta waves occur when a person is alert.
- C. Alpha waves occur in a state of relaxation, rather than beta waves occur when a person is alert.
- D. Alpha waves occur in a state of relaxation, instead of waves occur when a person is alert.
- E. Alpha waves occur in a state of relaxation, as for beta waves occur when a person is alert.

Item 12.
- A. In addition, delta waves take place for sleep, but they can also occur dysfunctionally when the brain has been severely damaged.
- B. In addition, delta waves take place during sleep, but they can also occur dysfunctionally when the brain has been severely damaged.
- C. In addition, delta waves take place since sleep, but they can also occur dysfunctionally when the brain has been severely damaged.
- D. In addition, delta waves take place with sleep, but they can also occur dysfunctionally when the brain has been severely damaged.
- E. In addition, delta waves take place at sleep, but they can also occur dysfunctionally when the brain has been severely damaged.

Item 13.
- A. Finally, theta waves are a frequency of
- B. Finally, theta waves are of a frequency
- C. Finally, theta waves of are a frequency
- D. Finally, of theta waves are a frequency
- E. Finally, theta waves are a of frequency

Item 14.
- A. somewhere in between alpha and delta.
- B. somewhere with between alpha and delta.
- C. somewhere in besides alpha and delta.
- D. somewhere at between alpha and delta.
- E. somewhere at besides alpha and delta.

Item 15.
A. Seems that the purpose of theta waves is solely to facilitate the combination of the other brain waves.
B. Seemingly that the purpose of theta waves is solely to facilitate the combination of the other brain waves.
C. It seemingly that the purpose of theta waves is solely to facilitate the combination of the other brain waves.
D. It is seemingly that the purpose of theta waves is solely to facilitate the combination of the other brain waves.
E. It seems that the purpose of theta waves is solely to facilitate the combination of the other brain waves.

Item 16.
A. The whole notion of brain waves feeds into the current controversy about brain death.
B. The whole notion of brain waves feeds at the current controversy about brain death.
C. The whole notion of brain waves feeds with the current controversy about brain death.
D. The whole notion of brain waves feeds against the current controversy about brain death.
E. The whole notion of brain waves feeds for the current controversy about brain death.

Item 17.
A. Some believe that brain death is characterized by the failure of the cerebral cortex to function.
B. Some people's belief that brain death is characterized by the failure of the cerebral cortex to function.
C. Some peoples' belief that brain death is characterized by the failure of the cerebral cortex to function.
D. Certain peoples believe that brain death is characterized by the failure of the cerebral cortex to function.
E. Certain believe that brain death is characterized by the failure of the cerebral cortex to function.

Item 18.
A. On the other hand, anothers say that mere damage to the cerebral cortex is not enough.
B. On the other hand, another say that mere damage to the cerebral cortex is not enough.
C. On the other hand, others say that mere damage to the cerebral cortex is not enough.
D. On the other hand, other say that mere damage to the cerebral cortex is not enough.
E. On the other hand, other's say that mere damage to the cerebral cortex is not enough.

Item 19.
A. They assert that brain stem function must also cease before can a person be declared dead because the cerebral cortex is responsible for other bodily processes.
B. They assert that brain stem function must also cease before a person can be declared dead because the cerebral cortex is responsible for other bodily processes.
C. They assert that brain stem function must also cease before may a person be declared dead because the cerebral cortex is responsible for other bodily processes.
D. They assert that brain stem function must also cease before might a person can be declared dead because the cerebral cortex is responsible for other bodily processes.
E. They assert that brain stem function must also cease before a person declared dead because the cerebral cortex is responsible for other bodily processes.

Item 20.
Imagine that the student would like to add the following sentence to the essay. What is the best location for this sentence?
Therefore, for these myriad reasons, it has become very important to measure brain activity.
        A.   At the end of the first paragraph.
        B.   At the end of the second paragraph.
        C.   At the end of the third paragraph.
        D.   At the beginning of the last paragraph.
        E.   At the end of the last paragraph.

ESSAY CORRECTION EXERCISE 5

[1] Cancer, a group of mainly than 100 different types of disease, [2] occurs where cells in the body begin to divide abnormally and continue dividing and forming more cells without control or order. [3] All internal organs of the body consist of cells, which normally divide to produce more cells when the body requires them. [4] This is a natural, orderly process, that keeps human beings healthy.

[5] If a cell divides when is not necessary, a large growth called a tumor can form. [6] These tumors can usually be removed, and in many cases, they do not recurrence. [7] Unfortunately, in some cases the cancer at the original tumor spreads. [8] The spread of cancer in such way is called metastasis.

[9] There are some factors which are being known to increase the risk of cancer. [10] Smoking is the single cause largest of death from cancer in the United States. [11] One-third of the death's from cancer each year are related to smoking, [12] making tobacco use the most preventable cause of death in this country.

[13] Choice of food can also be link to cancer. [14] Research shows that there are a link between high-fat food and certain cancers, and being seriously overweight is also a cancer risk. [15] Cancer risk can be reduced with a cut down on fatty food and eating generous amounts of fruit and vegetables.

Item 1.
        A.   Cancer, a group of mainly than 100 different types of disease,
        B.   Cancer, a group of more than 100 different types of disease,
        C.   Cancer, a group of 100 more different types of disease,
        D.   Cancer, a group of mostly than 100 different types of disease,
        E.   Cancer, a group of almost than 100 different types of disease,

Item 2.
        A.   occurs where cells in the body begin to divide abnormally and continue dividing and forming more cells without control or order.
        B.   occurs which cells in the body begin to divide abnormally and continue dividing and forming more cells without control or order.
        C.   occurs in which cells in the body begin to divide abnormally and continue dividing and forming more cells without control or order.
        D.   occurs when cells in the body begin to divide abnormally and continue dividing and forming more cells without control or order.
        E.   occurs once when cells in the body begin to divide abnormally and continue dividing and forming more cells without control or order.

Item 3.
- A. All internal organs of the body consist of cells, which normally divide to produce more cells when the body requires them.
- B. All internal organs of the body consist of cells, which divide to normally produce more cells when the body requires them.
- C. All internal organs of the body consist of cells, which divide to produce more normally cells when the body requires them.
- D. All internal organs of the body consist of cells, which divide to produce more cells when normally the body requires them.
- E. All internal organs of the body consist of cells, which divide to produce more cells when the body requires them normally.

Item 4.
- A. This is a natural, orderly process, that keeps human beings healthy.
- B. This is a natural, orderly process that keeps human beings healthy.
- C. This is a natural orderly process, that keeps human beings healthy.
- D. This is a natural orderly process that keeps human beings healthy.
- E. This is a natural orderly, process that keeps human beings healthy.

Item 5.
- A. If a cell divides when is not necessary, a large growth called a tumor can form.
- B. If a cell divides when they are not necessary, a large growth called a tumor can form.
- C. If a cell divides when it is not necessary, a large growth called a tumor can form.
- D. If a cell divides when are not necessary, a large growth called a tumor can form.
- E. If a cell divides when that not necessary, a large growth called a tumor can form.

Item 6.
- A. These tumors can usually be removed, and in many cases, they do not recurrence.
- B. These tumors can usually be removed, and in many cases, they do not make recurrence.
- C. These tumors can usually be removed, and in many cases, they do not recurring.
- D. These tumors can usually be removed, and in many cases, they do not are recurred.
- E. These tumors can usually be removed, and in many cases, they do not recur.

Item 7.
- A. Unfortunately, in some cases the cancer at the original tumor spreads.
- B. Unfortunately, in some cases the cancer from the original tumor spreads.
- C. Unfortunately, in some cases the cancer with the original tumor spreads.
- D. Unfortunately, in some cases the cancer for the original tumor spreads.
- E. Unfortunately, in some cases the cancer below the original tumor spreads.

Item 8.
- A. The spread of cancer in such way is called metastasis.
- B. The spread of cancer in such a way is called metastasis.
- C. The spread of cancer in such ways is called metastasis.
- D. The spread of cancer in such like way is called metastasis.
- E. The spread of cancer in such like ways is called metastasis.

Item 9.
- A. There are some factors which are being known to increase the risk of cancer.
- B. There are some factors which are know to increase the risk of cancer.
- C. There are some factors which are knowing to increase the risk of cancer.
- D. There are some factors which are known to increase the risk of cancer.
- E. There are some factors which have known to increase the risk of cancer.

Item.10
- A. Smoking is the single cause largest of death from cancer in the United States.
- B. Smoking is the single cause of largest death from cancer in the United States.
- C. Smoking is the single cause of death largest from cancer in the United States.
- D. Smoking is the single cause of death from cancer largest in the United States.
- E. Smoking is the largest single cause of death from cancer in the United States.

Item 11.
- A. One-third of the death's from cancer each year are related to smoking,
- B. One-third of the deaths' from cancer each year are related to smoking,
- C. One-third of the deaths from cancer each year are related to smoking,
- D. One-third of cancer's deaths each year are related to smoking,
- E. One-third of cancers' deaths each year are related to smoking,

Item 12.
- A. making tobacco use the most preventable cause of death in this country.
- B. which making tobacco use the most preventable cause of death in this country.
- C. made tobacco use the most preventable cause of death in this country.
- D. which will be making tobacco use the most preventable cause of death in this country.
- E. in making tobacco use the most preventable cause of death in this country.

Item 13.
- A. Choice of food can also be link to cancer.
- B. Choice of food can also be linking to cancer.
- C. Choice of food can also be linked to cancer.
- D. Choice of food can also been linked to cancer.
- E. Choice of food can also link to cancer.

Item 14.
- A. Research shows that there are a link between high-fat food and certain cancers, and being seriously overweight is also a cancer risk.
- B. Research shows that there is a link between high-fat food and certain cancers, and being seriously overweight is also a cancer risk.
- C. Research shows that there's links between high-fat food and certain cancers, and being seriously overweight is also a cancer risk.
- D. Research shows that there is existing a link between high-fat food and certain cancers, and being seriously overweight is also a cancer risk.
- E. Research shows that there in existence a link between high-fat food and certain cancers, and being seriously overweight is also a cancer risk.

Item 15.
- A. Cancer risk can be reduced with a cut down on fatty food and eating generous amounts of fruit and vegetables.
- B. Cancer risk can be reduced with cutting down on fatty food and eating generous amounts of fruit and vegetables.
- C. Cancer risk can be reduced with cutting down fatty food and eating generous amounts of fruit and vegetables.
- D. Cancer risk can be reduced by cutting down on fatty food and eating generous amounts of fruit and vegetables.
- E. Cancer risk can be reduced by cut down on fatty food and eating generous amounts of fruit and vegetables.

Item 16.
Suppose the student wants to include an admonition to the reader about how he or she can prevent cancer risks. Which sentence, if added to the end of the essay, would achieve this purpose?
- A. Accordingly, the government needs to act now to help improve the health of the country.
- B. Militating against the causes of cancer is a difficult but necessary task.
- C. It is therefore the responsibility of each individual to try to mitigate cancer risk by living a healthy lifestyle.
- D. However, these deaths could easily have been avoided.
- E. Nevertheless, most people agree that trying to prevent cancer risk is extremely important.

ANSWERS AND EXPLANATIONS

READING PRACTICE SET 1

1. The correct answer is B. The primary purpose of the first paragraph is to explain the basic tenets of Marxism, before going on to discuss Marxist views on capitalism and the consequences of private capital. We know this because the second sentence begins with the phrase "according to Marxism." Answer A is too general, and answers C and D are too specific.

2. The correct answer is D. The first two paragraphs give the background to the topic in a general way, and the second two paragraphs provide specific details about the topic. You may be tempted to choose answer C, but the criticism is only one aspect of the information provided in paragraph 4.

3. The correct answer is D. The writer mentions the "huge impact" that these writings have had on culture and politics in the last sentence in order to juxtapose this impact to Marx's failure to include pragmatic instructions in his work. We know that the author is making a juxtaposition or comparison because the sentence begins with the word "yet."

4. The correct answer is C. The word "commodious" means spacious. This is in contrast to the word "small" at the beginning of the sentence.

5. The correct answer is A. The second locomotive that Stephenson invented was an improvement on his first because it ran with greater force and speed. The last sentence of the passage states that "Stephenson's second 'iron horse' was even faster and more powerful than his first creation."

6. The correct answer is B. From the information contained in the passage, it seems reasonable to infer that George Stephenson's inventions laid the basic foundations for modern day public trains and railways. The passage describes how George Stephenson invented the steam locomotive and the world's first public railway. Such inventions lay the basic foundations, which can later be improved upon with advances in technology.

7. The correct answer is A. It can be inferred that patients today would most likely respond to treatments of the past with fear. We can assume that burning the skin was feared because it is described as a "so-called" treatment. In addition, the second sentence of paragraph 2 implies that these treatments were inhumane.

8. The correct answer is C. The primary purpose of the passage is to discuss Pasteur's discovery of the rabies vaccine. Paragraphs 1 and 2 focus on Pasteur's research on rabies. Paragraph 3 describes how the discovery of the rabies vaccine was made.

9. The correct answer is D. The passage suggests that the discovery of the rabies vaccine was significant because it helped many people avoid physical suffering and death. We know this because paragraph 1 explains that patients with rabies would suffer from "convulsions and delirium, and it would be too late to administer any remedy." The phrase "too late to administer any remedy" indicates that the patient would die from the infection.

10. The correct answer is D. The closest example to the use of a vaccine, as it is described in the passage, is children who get injections to prevent catching mumps and measles. It is the only example from the answer choices involving taking medicine beforehand in order to prevent catching a disease.

11. The correct answer is B. In the past, countries did not have constitutions or other established means to regulate the declaration of martial law. The third paragraph explains that "the constitutions of many countries now make provisions for the introduction of martial law." The use of the word "now" suggests that these provisions were not in place in the past.

12. The correct answer is A. It can be inferred from the passage that the United States Secretary of State would agree with the statement that the declaration of martial law is sometimes needed, although it usually undesirable. We know this because the last sentence of the passage states that, according to the United States Secretary of State, martial law is a "necessary albeit inimical outcome." "Inimical" means undesirable or unfavorable.

13. The correct answer is C. The last sentence of the second paragraph states that a coup is "defined as an illegal and usually violent seizure of a government by a select group of individuals." The use of the word "violent" suggests that other people may be killed or harmed.

14. The correct answer is D. The author finds fault with the civil order control function for its failure to answer the question: "Why do democratic nations sometimes deploy the military to impose order on their populations?" In paragraph 1, the writer explains that "the civil order control function suggests that public order is best maintained through agencies other than the police force or militia." However, the writer explains in paragraph 4 that "in spite of these democratic systems being in place, forms of military control are still instituted during times of crisis, with a country's military system being mobilized to support civil authorities, such as municipalities and local police forces."

15. The correct answer is D. It can be inferred that the author of the passage would agree with the basic tenet of the civil order control function because there are occasions when public order can only be reinstated through the establishment of military rule, in spite of the disadvantages in doing so. In paragraph 1, the author writes that "martial law, the establishment of military rule over a civilian population, is only imposed when other methods of civil control have proven ineffective." So, the author believes that martial law should only be used when the civil order control function, which is usually the best option, has failed.

16. The correct answer is A. When reading poetry, it is normal to slow down your reading rate in order to understand the poetic language that is used in the text.

17. The correct answer is C. The last stanza of the poem says: "And fare thee weel awhile! And I will come again, my luve." "Fare thee weel" means farewell, which is the same as a goodbye. Then the poet says he will come again, so we know that he is leaving, but that he will not be gone forever.

18. The correct answer is D. In the second stanza, the poet says: "So fair art thou, my bonnie lass." *Fair* is an old-fashioned word for beautiful, so we can surmise that *bonnie* has a similar meaning. *Pretty* is the closest synonym for *beautiful*, so D is the correct answer.

19. The correct answer is A. In the first paragraph, the author suggests that our mental and physiological sense of time is appropriate. The author explains that all human beings have this sense of time. The author does not criticize this behavior, but rather, provides factual information about the topic. From the tone of the passage, we can therefore surmise that that author views this behavior as appropriate.

20. The correct answer is B. In the first sentence of paragraph 4, the phrase "these cycles" refers to circadian rhythms. The two previous sentences state: "Circadian rhythms help to explain the "lark vs. owl" hypothesis. Larks are those who quite rightly prefer to rise early in the morning and go to bed early, while owls are those who feel at their best at night and stay up too late." Larks and owls are given as an example, so the phrase "these rhythms" refers back to the subject of circadian rhythms in the previous sentence.

21. The correct answer is A. The author's attitude toward owls in the "lark vs. owl" hypothesis can best be described as one of disapproval. The author says that larks "quite rightly prefer to rise early in the morning," but owls "stay up too late." So, the author disapproves of the owl's behavior.

22. The correct answer is D. The author would most likely recommend that sufferers of jet lag allow their body clocks to adjust to the time difference naturally. The author begins the third paragraph by explaining that "these natural rhythms, sometimes called circadian rhythms, are partially controlled by the hypothalamus in the brain." Since the author refers to the rhythms as a natural phenomenon, he or she would most likely suggest that the time difference be overcome naturally.

23. The correct answer is C. For questions asking you about the order of steps or events, you need to focus on the part of the passage where the particular step is mentioned. Here, we can see that the question is asking about the occurrence of pressure on the tectonic plates. So, we need to focus on the last two sentences of the first paragraph: "The two plates will eventually shift or separate because the pressure on them is constantly increasing, and this build-up of energy needs to be released. When the plates shift or separate, we have an occurrence of an earthquake, also known as a seismic event." You also need to pay attention to the words in the question that are indicating the sequencing, such as "before," "after," "next," or "during." The question asks us: "What happens immediately after the pressure on the tectonic plates has become too great?" The word "after" shows that we need to determine the next step. The passage indicates that after the pressure builds up, it needs to be released. The passage states that the release of energy in this way causes an earthquake, which is also called "a seismic event." So, answer C is correct.

24. The correct answer is D. In order to draw an inference, you should make only a small logical step based on the information contained in the passage. Try to avoid making wild guesses. In this passage, we see that the sentence to be placed in the gap mentions that lives can be saved through prediction systems, while the last sentence states that "these prediction systems need to be more reliable in order to be of any practical use." Accordingly, we can surmise that at the time the passage was written, prediction systems were not reliable enough. Therefore, not as many lives were being saved as would have been possible if the systems had been more reliable.

25. The correct answer is A. For questions about the author's persuasive technique or strategies, you should focus on the sentences before the one that contains the final direct statement by the author. In this passage, the author's final direct statement is that "these prediction systems need to be more reliable in order to be of any practical use." The author's final statement is dispassionate because she precedes it with the scientific descriptions of earthquake waves and epicenters. Note that "dispassionate" means objective or stated without strong emotion.

READING PRACTICE SET 2

1. The correct answer is D. It can be inferred from the passage that the primary reason why the court wizards performed magical illusions was to make Kublai Khan and his court appear powerful and mysterious. The second paragraph uses the words "amazement" and "astonishing" to express the mysteriousness of the court.

2. The correct answer is C. The author most probably uses the word "levitate" in paragraph 2 to mean hover. The words "levitate" and "hover" both mean to be suspended in midair.

3. The correct answer is B. Some academics find fault with *Il Milione* for its failure to answer the following question: Why should we believe Polo's version of events? The passage explains that "Although some academics have disputed the veracity of Polo's written account of the Khan Empire, common sense tells us that there would have been little motive for the explorer to have exaggerated his version of events." The phrase "dispute the veracity" means that they doubt whether the story is true.

4. The correct answer is D. The passage gives the historical background to a piece of writing and then provides further details about it. Paragraphs 1 and 2 describe the book *Il Milione*, and paragraphs 3 and 4 provide some additional information about Polo's written account of events.

5. The correct answer is D. The author would most likely agree with the statement that Cleopatra's use of cosmetics reflected the fashion of the times in which she lived. The last sentence of paragraph 1 mentions that "Cleopatra wore blue eye shadow made of ground lapis lazuli stone, much like other women of her day."

6. The correct answer is A. The first paragraph provides one example, while the second paragraph gives further examples. The entire passage talks about cosmetics. Paragraph 1 talks about eye shadow, and paragraph 2 describes other cosmetics, such as eye liner, lip and cheek color, and nail polish.

7. The correct answer is C. The passage is expository because it merely provides information on cosmetics in ancient times, without taking a particular position on the topic.

8. The correct answer is A. The passage is primarily concerned with describing the history of dance notation and its use. The theme of the passage is introduced in the last sentence of the first paragraph, which says that "more than one hundred systems of dance notation have been created over the past few centuries." The phrase "past few centuries" indicates that a historical account is going to be given.

9. The correct answer is B. The function of the first sentence of the passage is to set up relevant analogies. An analogy is a comparison. The passage compares dance notation to written scores and written scripts.

10. The correct answer is A. According to the passage, Beauchamp-Feuillet notation differs from Vladimir Ivanovich Stepanov's notation system in that Stepanov's system was used for a different genre of dance during a different time period. Stepanov's system was used for ballet after the eighteenth century. The system that Pierre Beauchamp devised was used for Baroque dance until the end of the eighteenth century.

11. The correct answer is C. The passage indicates that Hanya Holm was the first person to register intellectual property rights for a dance notation system. Paragraph 3 states that "Hanya Holm was the first choreographer to copyright the notations of her dance scores." Copyright is a kind of intellectual property right.

12. The correct answer is D. The author most likely mentions Apple and other computerized dance notation systems in the last sentence of the passage in order to indicate possible trends in dance notation. We know this because the sentence focuses on new developments in dance notation.

13. The correct answer is B. The concept of synchronous rotation, as it is defined in the passage, provides the most likely explanation for the situation in which a telecommunications satellite is always in the same position above a certain city on Earth. This is similar to the way in which the same hemisphere of the Moon always faces the Earth.

14. The correct answer is D. Point 5 in paragraph 3 states that the last step in lunar evolution was "the cessation of volcanic activity followed by gradual internal cooling." So, we can conclude that after lunar evolution, the temperature of the internal core of the Moon was lower than it was previously.

15. The correct answer is A. An analysis revealing that there are no geological similarities between samples of material from the surface of the Moon and material from the Earth's crust would tend to disprove the hypothesis that the Moon grew out of debris that was dislodged from the Earth's crust. If we assume that the Moon grew out of material from the Earth, we would expect to see some geological similarities.

16. The correct answer is B. "*These differences*" refers to the phrase "variations in soil composition" which is mentioned in the previous sentence in paragraph 4.

17. The correct answer is D. Paragraph 2 states: "A logical locality to begin searching is one near sites in which artifacts have been found previously."

18. The correct answer is D. The meaning of this word is revealed in the next sentence in paragraph 5: "the mechanism goes back and forth in this way . . ."

19. The correct answer is A. Sentence 2 of paragraph 6 states that cataloging "can certainly be tedious; yet, it is one that is critical in order to account for each and every item properly." The phrase "account for" means to be sure that every item is present, or stated conversely, to be sure that no item is missing.

20. The correct answer is C. The last sentence of paragraph 7 states: "Unfortunately, as a consequence, the misapprehension that the origins of homo sapiens were European began to take shape both in the archeological and wider communities." The word "unfortunately" makes it clear that this action is regrettable. The words "misunderstanding" and "misapprehension" are synonyms. The phrase "wider communities" means culturally.

21. The correct answer is C. The first sentence of paragraph 8 states: "social and cultural biases pervaded the manner in which archeological findings were investigated and explicated during the early nineteenth century . . ." "Pervade" means to affect extensively. "Explicate" means explain.

22. The correct answer is A. The last paragraph states: "By the middle of the 1900's, [. . .] there was a surge in artifacts excavated from African and Asian localities." Since there was a surge or sudden increase in the discovery of artifacts from Asia and Africa around the 1950's, we can conclude that there were few archeological findings from these areas previously.

23. The correct answer is C. The article discusses the three main ideas stated in choice C. The following statement in choices A and D is false according to the article: "The European archeological discoveries of the 1800s should be disregarded." The other ideas mentioned in choices A, B, and D are true according to the article, but they are specific points, not main ideas. Artifact interpretation and Darwinian theory are archeological developments, not archeological field methods.

24. The correct answer is D. The metallurgical composition of a coin is determined to be correct by the electricity that has passed through the magnet. Paragraph 2 states: "Electricity passes through the magnet, causing the coin to slow down in some cases. If the coin begins to slow down, its metallurgic composition has been deemed to be correct." That is to say, the coin slows down because of the electricity that has passed through the magnet.

25. The correct answer is B. The last step in testing the coin is the determination of its metallurgic composition. This step is provided in the last sentence of paragraph 2: "If the coin begins to slow down, its metallurgic composition has been deemed to be correct." Be careful if you chose answer D. The deflector is not a step in the testing process, but rather an alternative outcome of the test.

READING PRACTICE SET 3

1. The correct answer is D. The last paragraph mentions that "the acid in rain also emanates from automobile exhaust, domestic residences, and power stations. The latter have been the culprit of the bulk of the acid in rainwater in recent years." The phrase "the latter" refers to the last thing mentioned, so it refers to power stations at the end of the previous sentence. Therefore, power stations have been the largest contributor to the problem.

2. The correct answer is A. The mention of the chemicals nitrogen and sulfur in paragraph 2 shows that a scientific explanation is being provided. Paragraph 3 talks about "exacerbating the problem," indicating that current problems are being discussed. Accordingly, the organization of the passage is scientific explanation and current problems.

3. The correct answer is C. The statement that best supports the writer's main idea is that "the effect of the structures has been to spread the gases more thinly and widely in the atmosphere, thereby exacerbating the problem." This statement links back to the main idea of the passage, which is stated in paragraph 1, sentence 2: "scientific research shows that the acid content of rain has increased dramatically over the past two hundred years, in spite of humanity's recent attempts to control the problem."

4. The correct answer is C. For main idea questions, look to see which ideas are stated in each part of the passage. The first half of this passage addresses economics, while the second half talks about the environment. The central idea of the passage is therefore that organic farming has become one of the fastest growing trends in agriculture recently not only for monetary, but also for environmental reasons. This is the only answer that expresses both of the ideas. The other answers are merely restating specific points from the passage.

5. The correct answer is D. In order to identify the style of a passage, you need to examine the transitional words and phrases in the passage. We can see that reasons and explanations are given in the passage, using the phrases "not only," "but also," and "that is because." Accordingly, the writing style is explanatory.

6. The correct answer is A. The tanks are protected against leaks because they are encased in concrete. The fourth sentence of paragraph one states: "For extra protection, the tanks are double-walled and surrounded by a concrete covering that is one meter thick."

7. The correct answer is B. The first two sentences of paragraph one introduce the idea of radioactive waste generally, before moving on to talk about how the waste is stored at the present time, so the best title for paragraph one is "Current Storage Solutions for Radioactive Waste." Paragraph two begins by discussing the problems with storing the waste in this way and ends by giving an overview of possible solutions to these problems, so "Potential Problems and Long-Term Solutions" is the best title for paragraph two.

8. The correct answer is D. The author implies that a radioactive leak would have dire consequences since he opens the passage with this sentence: "Highly concentrated radioactive waste is lethal and can remain so for thousands of years."

9. The correct answer is D. We need to have a look at the first and second sentences of the last paragraph, which state: "The artists utilized ochre and manganese as engraving tools in order first to etch their outlines on the walls of the caves. Before removing their lamps and leaving their creations to dry, they painted the walls with brushes of animal hair or feathers." Be sure to read sentences like these very carefully. The etching is the first step. The application of the paint is the second step. Removing the lamps is the third step, while leaving the paint to dry is the final step.

10. The correct answer is B. The attitude of the writer is that it is amazing that Stone Age artists were able to paint such beautiful creations in spite of the extreme conditions they faced. For questions like this one, look for adjectives in the passage that give hints about the author's point of view. The phrase "stunning drawings" in paragraph 1 indicates the author's amazement.

11. The correct answer is C. Paragraph 3 focuses on the natural elements that were used in the process of creating the drawings. Therefore, this sentence is least relevant to the main idea since it de-emphasizes the importance of certain natural elements.

12. The correct answer is B. The use of quotations in the passage suggests that the followers of Noh are traditional, discerning, and serious. Paragraphs 1 and 2 use quotation marks when they state that Noh is for the "discriminating Japanese aristocracy" and that it depicts a "solemn act." The word "aristocracy"

indicates that the dance is traditional in nature. "Discriminating" means "discerning," and "solemn" means "serious."

13. The correct answer is A. The last paragraph implies that Japanese audiences today would respond to Kabuki theater with admiration. The last sentence of the last paragraph states: "Because of its appeal to the general populace, Kabuki theater remains as fascinating and exotic as it has always been." We can surmise that people probably admire something that fascinates them.

14. The correct answer is D. Followers of Noh and followers of Kabuki would probably agree that Japanese theater is an important and interesting aspect of Japanese culture. The first sentence of the passage explains that these forms of theater "have emerged from Japanese culture." Since an article has been devoted to this topic, we can assume that followers consider the topic to be an important and interesting aspect of the Japanese culture.

15. The correct answer is C. Paragraphs 1 to 4 talk about "a new project [that] is underway to assist colleges that train students to teach vocational subjects" (paragraph 2).

16. The correct answer is D. Paragraph 2 states: "The first 30 teacher trainees are to commence work later this month. Unlike previous teachers in training, these students, who want to teach vocational subjects like construction and photography, will not have to waste time by composing essays."

See the chart below for the answers. Support for these answers can be found in paragraph 4 of the lecture.

Details of Edge Foundation Program for New Teachers
17. Greater emphasis on teaching *vocational* subjects.
18. Employers were requesting *better* teachers.
19. New courses will emphasize teaching, especially in the teacher's *subject*.
20. Each teacher trainee will receive help from a *mentor*.

21. The correct answer is B. Paragraph 6 states that "results for ethnic minority children are rising faster than the average. Thus, what is needed is a far more plural system." "Plural" is synonymous with "diverse."

22. The correct answers are A and E. Paragraph 7 tells us that the system needs to "ensure that there is no devaluation of academic standards and college graduates have the skills required for a more competitive job market."

23. The correct answer is C. Paragraph 8 explains: "Governmental officials on the Education Select Committee will suggest that some of the cash might be better directed to making buildings more environmentally sustainable . . . or boosting pre-school learning."

24. The correct answer is B. Paragraph 9 states: "The report on the Building Schools for the Future (BSF) program . . . says the scheme must be regularly reviewed."

25. The correct answer is D. Paragraph 9 points out that local authorities have complained that "the government may force them into becoming private academies as part of BSF."

READING PRACTICE SET 4

1. The correct answer is C. The sentence before this one states that "a funnel is produced that extends from the cloud above it to the earth below." So, we know that the funnel hangs from the cloud.

2. The correct answer is D. The phrase "creates a path of destruction" refers to an event that causes extensive damage. The word "landscape" in this sentence refers to the countryside in a particular geographic region. The word "landscaped" in the answer choices is used to describe lawns and gardens.

3. The correct answer is D. Paragraph 4 states that tornadoes cause 70 deaths each year in the US. It also states that tornadoes "usually occur between 3:00 PM and 9:00 PM." Finally, the paragraph mentions that tornadoes are most common during the summer. Wind speed is not mentioned until paragraph 5.

4. The correct answer is C. Because of the phrase "normally classified" in the same sentence, we know that we are making a general rule based on *many* individual events of tornadoes.

5. The correct answer is A. The author's purpose is stated in the first two sentences of this paragraph: "Tornadoes are normally classified as weak, strong, or violent. It is notable that the majority of all tornadoes are categorized as weak."

6. The correct answer is B. Paragraph 6 states: "For example, some people hold the view that tornadoes cannot occur over oceans, lakes, or rivers. However, waterspouts, tornadoes that develop over bodies of water, can in many cases cause major damage to coastal areas as they move onshore." So, we can see that this is an example of misinformation. The idea of misinformation is also mentioned in paragraph1, which states that "very few people actually understand how these weather events occur."

7. The correct answer is D. Paragraph 6 talks about myths and misconceptions. Both of these words mean that people do not possess factual information about a certain topic.

8. The correct answer is C. Paragraph 7 states: "Cars and other vehicles offer very little protection when tornadoes hit, so drivers should leave their vehicles and look for safe shelter. Mobile homes and trailers also afford little shelter, so residents of these types of dwellings should go to an underground floor of the nearest building." The basement is the underground floor of a building.

9. The correct answer is D. The article mainly discusses the loss of life and property caused by tornadoes. Answer choices A, B, and C are specific points from the article.

10. The correct answer is A. The article mentions the two ideas summarized in answer choice A. The other information in answer choices B, C, and D is mentioned in the article as specific points, not main ideas.

11. The correct answer is A. The mention of "nine scenes" in answer A relates to the phrase "the scenes" at the start of the next sentence.

12. The correct answer is C. Michelangelo dismissed his assistants because he believed that they were inept craftsmen. See the last sentence of paragraph 1, which states that "as work proceeded, the artist dismissed each of his assistants one by one, claiming that they lacked the competence necessary to do the task at hand."

13. The correct answer is D. The following sentence expresses a claim of the author rather than a fact: "Yet, he went on to paint one of the most beautiful works in art history." The adjectival phrase "the most beautiful" indicates that a claim is being given.

14. The correct answer is D. The writer of passage 1 speaks out against credit card debt, so she would disagree with the following statement from passage 2: "My philosophy is to set out to find the best prices I can get on quantity purchases of such things as bathroom items and dry and canned food, even if I have to use my credit card to get them."

15. The correct answer is B. The writer of passage 2 would disagree with the statement that "the real cause of your financial mess is you" because she asserts that "external forces and market conditions have a huge impact on personal financial situations."

16. The correct answer is C. We know that the narrator is talking about the wallpaper because she is describing the patterns on the paper. She then goes on to talk about the wallpaper in the majority of the passage.

17. The correct answer is A. For emphasis questions like this one, think about how the statement would sound if spoken aloud. The word "reason" would be emphasized if the narrator were speaking in a sarcastic way. The narrator also talks about the way in which the conclusion that she is not being reasonable satisfies her husband. She is talking about the situation from his point of view, not hers, so she is implying that he thinks she is irrational.

18. The correct answer is B. The passage mentions various ways in which the narrator's husband will not accommodate her wishes, so the reader can assume that their relationship is difficult or strained.

19. The correct answer is C. The narrator speaks about nervousness, which she uses as a euphemism for nervous breakdown or depression. She states at the beginning of paragraph 3: "These nervous troubles are dreadfully depressing."

20. The correct answer is D. Her husband's opinion is that it is fanciful or whimsical to put up new wallpaper for a short-term lease.

21. The correct answer is B. The narrator talks about a ship, his captivity, and being in an isolated condition, so we can surmise that he is stranded on a deserted island.

22. The correct answer is C. "Victual" is an antiquated word meaning food. We can understand this from the context of the passage because the narrator talks about putting bread, rice, and meat on the ship.

23. The correct answer is A. The narrator is being sarcastic. He is stranded and alone, so there is no one over whom he can reign.

24. The correct answer is D. "Reproach" means scold; "unthankful temper" means not appreciating what one has; "solitary condition" means loneliness, and the utterance "what I would give to be on shore there again" means that he wants to go back to the island.

25. The correct answer is A. The statement "we never see the true state of our condition till it is illustrated to us by its contraries" would be expressed in present-day English as "you don't know what you've got until it's gone."

READING PRACTICE SET 5

1. The correct answer is C. Paragraph 1 states the main idea of these paragraphs: "movie stars who regularly smoke in films are influencing young people to smoke cigarettes."

2. The correct answer is C. Paragraph 4 states: "The WHO survey found that 76% of the most popular films produced worldwide within the last ten years showed some form of tobacco use." You may be

tempted to choose answer A. However, 65% represents the number of actors who are portrayed smoking in movies.

3. The correct answer is B. In paragraph 4, we read that "the WHO's World No Tobacco Day focuses on how the fashion and film industries glamorize cigarettes."

4. The correct answer is D. This sentence in paragraph 4 gives the most significant idea of the paragraph: "This research shows a clear relation between on-screen tobacco use by movie stars and higher levels of beginning to smoke by the teenagers who admire them." The other answers provide information that merely supports the main, significant finding.

5. The correct answers are B, C, and E. The information to support these answers is in paragraphs 4, 7, and 8.

6. The correct answer is C. The blame is shifted in the following comment: "One leading film-maker said tobacco companies, not movie stars, were to blame for teenage smoking."

7. The correct answer is A. We can understand that paragraph 8 is providing statistics because of the number of percentages and other figures it includes.

8. The correct answer is B. According to Dr. Edward Adams, the increase in experimental smoking is accompanied by an increase in that of regular smoking. Paragraph 9 states: "The rise in those experimenting with smoking has been matched by an increase in regular smokers as well."

9. The correct answer is B. Paragraph 10 points out that children who "showed signs of being hooked only had an average of two cigarettes a week. Some of these kids were hooked within a few days of starting to smoke."

10. The correct answer is C. Paragraph 10 states: "His team suggested that brains of adolescents, because they were still growing, were more vulnerable to addiction. The effect of tobacco might be stronger and longer lasting than in adults."

11. The correct answer is D. General information about the research is provided, and then the specific findings of the research are presented. The first two paragraphs describe the background to archeological research in Africa, and the second two paragraphs give specific details about the remains and artifacts that were discovered there.

12. The correct answer is D. The author states that "genetic science confirms that these are quite likely the oldest remains in the world of modern people" in paragraph 2 primarily in order to emphasize the significance of archeological discoveries in Africa. We know this because the paragraph goes on to explain that "these findings are more than sufficient in order to make a number of significant conclusions."

13. The correct answer is D. As used in paragraph 3, the word "variation" most likely means variety. "Variation" is synonymous with the words "wide array" and "diverse," which are used later in paragraph 2.

14. The correct answer is A. From the passage, it can be inferred that some of the archeological discoveries from Africa were broken into small pieces or extremely damaged. The last sentence of paragraph 2 of the passage tells us that "the artifacts and skeletons of early Africans are most commonly found in a highly fragmented state." "Fragmented" means broken into pieces.

15. The correct answer is B. The passage suggests that the discovery of microliths was significant because these tools demonstrate the level of sophistication and ingenuity of the prehistoric African population. The second to last sentence of paragraph 4 states: "Having been developed long before the

invention of metallurgy, tools had gradually become smaller and more sophisticated." Microliths are then given as an example of more sophisticated tools.

16. The correct answer is B. The passage explains how Mr. Morris conformed to social convention throughout his life. We can see this idea, for example, at the end of paragraph 1, which states: "Everything that it was right and proper for a man in his position to possess, he possessed." This idea is repeated at the beginning of paragraph 4, in the statement that: "He underwent various changes according to the accepted custom in these cases."

17. The correct answer is A. Paragraph 2 describes how Mr. Morris had "the right sort and number of children." So, the reader can assume that Mr. Morris's children, like Mr. Morris himself, conform to social convention by trying to be responsible and logical.

18. The correct answer is D. Something that is sham is used only for show or to impress others. Accordingly, the adjective "pretentious" from answer choice D is the best synonym for "sham."

19. The correct answer is C. The narrator tells us that Mr. Morris's home was "a nice sensible house," and his tomb is described as "being the fashion of his time." The reader can therefore deduce that both the house and the tomb would have been considered right and proper for the society of their time.

20. The correct answer is A. The reader can conclude that the story is going to be about how life in the future is different than life in the past because it talks about both the past and the future in the last paragraph of the passage. In addition, the word "future" is capitalized in one instance to give emphasis to this concept.

21. The correct answer is D. "He'd catch it" means that Oliver was to be punished. This interpretation is supported by paragraph 2, which implies that Mrs. Snowberry is an authoritarian whom the boys fear.

22. The correct answer is D. in the second paragraph of the text Charlotte states "I have saved a nice little bit of bacon for you from master's breakfast." In those days, the task of preparing meals and cleaning up after them would have been done by a servant, not a family member. Charlotte also refers to Mr. Snowberry as "master," so we know that she is a servant.

23. The correct answer is D. Noah exclaims about Oliver: "Let him alone!" This exclamation indicates that Oliver is the source of ridicule. The passage also mentions that Oliver is scorned, which is synonymous with being ridiculed.

24. The correct answer is D. The passage mainly illustrates the relationship between Noah and Oliver. This idea is illustrated especially clearly in the last paragraph of the passage, in which we see Noah's view of Oliver.

25. The correct answer is D. The last sentence of the passage states: "But now that fortune had cast his way a nameless orphan, at whom even the meanest could point the finger of scorn, he retorted on him with interest." In this sentence, "his" refers to Noah, so the "nameless orphan" must refer to Oliver.

READING PRACTICE SET 6

1. The correct answer is D. The passage uses phrases like "the response . . . is mixed," "many still resist," and "legally possible" to describe these debates.

2. The correct answer is C. Paragraph 1 states: "Scientists have been able to clone mice for the very first time by using stem cells harvested from the hairs of mature animals. The procedure is much more efficient than cloning with the use of adult cells."

3. The correct answer is D. Paragraph 2 explains that "If embryonic stem cells, which can turn into any type of tissue, were harvested from the early-stage embryo they could be used to regenerate damaged tissue which is genetically matched to a patient. This would avoid immune rejection." Answer choice A is incorrect because the embryos are not used directly as transplants; they only help to reproduce the tissue.

4. The correct answers are B and C. Paragraph 5 tells us that "Currently it is only legally possible to carry out two kinds of reproductive assistance on humans using In Vitro Fertilization to fertilize eggs outside the mother's body. The first procedure involves determining the genes and sex of the unborn baby. The second technique, called Pre-implantation Genetic Diagnosis, conducts embryo screening for genetic diseases."

5. The correct answer is B. Paragraph 7 argues that "its detractors insist that its defining feature is simply its larger size."

6. The correct answer is A. The final paragraph presents the following argument: "Even if we can change our lifestyles, will we do so? Many people may treat susceptibility-prediction as inevitability, and relapse into even worse lifestyles."

7. The correct answer is D. The two tools which were used to place the stones into their final positions on the pyramid were made from wood. Paragraph 3 mentions wooden rods and wooden rockers.

8. The correct answer is C. Between paragraphs 1 and 2, the writer's approach shifts from background information to specific details. Paragraph 1 describes tools in general, while paragraph 2 names specific tools.

9. The correct answer is C. The writer's main purpose is to give an overview of some of the main implements that were used to construct the Giza pyramids. The main purpose of the passage is implied in the last sentence of the first paragraph: "it is notable that the Egyptians had only the most primitive, handmade tools to complete the massive project.

10. The correct answer is A. The assumption that has most influenced the writer is that it is incredible that the Egyptians were able to construct the pyramids using only hand-made tools. The assumption that the outcome was incredible is shown by the contrast between the words "primitive" and "massive" in the last sentence of paragraph 1.

11. The correct answer is B. Paragraph 1 discusses the increase in popularity of the theory of multiple intelligences, while paragraph 2 gives further information on the theory of multiple intelligences, namely, some background information and a discussion of the educational implications. Therefore, answer B is the best because it is gives the general ideas of each paragraph. The other answers give only specific ideas from each of the paragraphs.

12. The correct answer is C. The last sentence talks about implications for teaching and learning, so the talk is being given in an education class.

13. The correct answer is D. The writer of passage 1 talks about office life in paragraph 1 and about business users in paragraph 2. The writer of passage 2 does not mention these aspects of wireless technology.

14. The correct answer is C. The writer of passage 2 explains how people are more inclined to stay at home to chat on social media than to go out with friends and how people are glued to their hand-held devices even when they are out with friends. These are two detrimental impacts of social media on interpersonal relationships.

15. The correct answer is C. The writer of passage 1 describes the positive changes, while the writer of passage 2 describes the negative changes.

16. The correct answer is A. The narrator states in paragraph 2 that he needs to spend the autumn "economically," so the reader can surmise that he is having financial problems. Note that the narrator mentions that he is "out of spirits," but this condition is not as serious as suffering from depression.

17. The correct answer is C. The narrator says: "It was one of the two evenings in every week which I was accustomed to spend with my mother and my sister." The word "accustomed" indicates that a routine is being described.

18. The correct answer is B. The doorman would have been the servant who welcomed visitors at the front door of the house.

19. The correct answer is D. "Collegial" means acting like colleagues, or people who work in the same profession. Paragraph 5 of the text explains that Professor Pesca and the narrator met when they were teachers, so the two characters would have been colleagues.

20. The correct answer is C. The last paragraph tells us that swimming was one of the "manly exercises which the Professor believed that he could learn impromptu." The word "impromptu" means "on the spot" or "without previous practice or experience."

21. The correct answer is C. The description moves from the roads, to the garden, and then to the house. In other words, the description moves from the outdoors to the house itself, so the bartonwalls are probably a part of the house.

22. The correct answer is D. Paragraph 1 mentions that it is after dusk and that it was nighttime. We also know from paragraph 1 that Clare was restless and that he had gone out.

23. The correct answer is A. "Mutual bearing" means how they interact with each other. "Third parties" is a formal way of saying "other people."

24. The correct answer is C. We know that the story takes place in a dairy farm because Clare confesses that he has fallen in love with a milkmaid at the end of paragraph 3.

25. The correct answer is D. In the next sentence of the paragraph, the narrator tells us that "Tess was no insignificant creature to toy with and dismiss; but a woman living her precious life—a life which, to herself who endured or enjoyed it, possessed as great a dimension as the life of the mightiest to himself." This sentence describes both the positive and negative experiences in Tess's life. It implies that Clare needs to respect Tess when it states that she "was no insignificant creature to toy with and dismiss."

EXTENDED READING PRACTICE SET 1

1. The correct answer is A. The theory described in paragraph 2 appeared in the first century. It is also described as "unformulated." For these reasons, we know that the theory was newly formed.

2. The correct answer is C. "Compatriot" means a person who has the same nationality as someone else. At the beginning of paragraph 2, Ptolemy is described as "another Greek scientist."

3. The correct answer is C. "Flash of inspiration" means that a single event caused a positive outcome. It is the opposite of the phrase "slowly developed over time." So, the law of gravity was created slowly.

4. The correct answer is D. The phrase "Newton must also be acknowledged for the realization that . . ." at the end of paragraph 5 emphasizes Newton's "prescience" or "realization."

5. The correct answer is D. Paragraph 5 mentions "geological features" so we know that A is true. Paragraph 5 also mentions "the declining mass and density of the planet from the equator" so we know that B is also true. Finally, Paragraph 5 mentions that "gravity becomes less robust [or not as strong] as the distance from the equator diminishes" so we know that C is true. D is incorrect because gravity influences rocks and geological features. The rocks do not influence gravity.

6. The correct answer is B. "Reservation" means confusion or doubt. It is close in meaning to the word "perplexed" and the phrase "unable adequately to explain."

7. The correct answer is A. Paragraph 7 states that "Einstein asserted that the paths of objects in motion can sometimes . . . change direction . . . as a result of the curvature of space time."

8. The correct answer is D. Paragraph 6 concludes by describing these hypotheses today. So, we must be speaking about the twenty-first century as mentioned in the new sentence.

9. The correct answer is B. Paragraph 7 states that Einstein's work was "revolutionary" and that it has been "unequivocally supported." Both of these statements describe positive reactions.

10. The correct answer is C. These are the three main ideas. The other items give specific details.

11. The correct answer is D. Notice that the word "average" is used five times in paragraph two. Look for word repetition like this as you try to find synonyms on the reading test.

12. The correct answer is A. "Disparity" means difference. "Enormous" means very large. So, the statistics given in paragraph 2 support statement A.

13. The correct answer is C. The passage uses words like "bifurcate" and "dichotomy" to talk about the division of the economy. The passage also talks about high and low levels of salary.

14. The correct answer is D. The grammatical subject of this clause in the sentence is "contribution." "Benefit" and "contribution" are near synonyms.

15. The correct answer is D. Paragraph 4 states that "Recently, cultural and critical theorists have joined in the economic debate", so A is correct. Paragraph 4 also states that "various forms of media promote the mechanisms of economic manipulation and oppression," so B is correct. Finally, paragraph 4 states that "those of lower socio-economic class . . . view themselves as . . . powerless victims." So C is also correct.

16. The correct answer is A. The word "noisome" means negative or harmful. The entire passage speaks about the negative effects of the present economic situation.

17. The correct answer is B. The phrase "a theoretical stance has recently sprung into existence" in paragraph 3 is similar in meaning to the phrase "burgeoning school of thought" in the new sentence.

18. The correct answer is B. "Poorer countries" is synonymous with "less economically advanced." "Peripheral" is similar in meaning to "irrelevant." Finally, "policy" is similar in meaning to "protocol."

19. The correct answer is C. The economic effects of social inequality is the main theme of this reading passage. So, the author wants to illustrate the main theme. The answers B and D are too strongly-worded and emphatic, and answer A is too specific.

20. The correct answer is C. The passage is speaking about the harm caused to low-paid people. Answers A, B, and D contain words with positive connotations.

21. The correct answer is A. This is the main idea from paragraph 4. Note that answer choice D exaggerates the consequence of early death.

22. The correct answer is B. Paragraph 6 states: "In order to solve this problem, many economists believe that consideration must be given not only to political arrangements . . . but also to the social interaction between people and groups." Answers A and C are incorrect because the paragraph describes both of these problems. Answer D is incorrect because the paragraph does not discuss the interaction between the political and social aspects.

23. The correct answer is C. The word "conversely" at the beginning of paragraph 7 indicates that there is a dispute or disagreement.

24. The correct answer is D. Paragraph 1 states: "Piaget determined that younger children responded to research questions differently than older children. His conclusion was that different responses occurred not because younger children were less intelligent, but because they were at a lower level of biological development." In other words, he linked their intellectual ability to their biological development.

25. The correct answer is C. "Coin a term" means to invent a new word or term.

26. The correct answer is D. Answer A is true because the first sentence of paragraph 2 talks about Piaget's work as a biologist. Answer B is true since the second sentence of paragraph 2 describes Piaget's discovery of mental schemes. Answer C is true because the last sentence of paragraph 2 provides details about environmental adaptation. The paragraph does not state that Piaget was the first researcher in this field, so choice D is not true.

27. The correct answer is A. The second sentence of this paragraph states that the sensorimotor stage is the first stage.

28. The correct answer is B. The next part of the sentence states that: "his or her intellectual and emotional energy is self-centered rather than empathetic." Self-centered is a synonym for selfish.

29. The correct answer is B. The schemes are mentioned for the first time in paragraph 3, so the new sentence needs to be placed in this paragraph.

30. The correct answer is C. The sentence mentions both the social environment and the idea of bifurcation, or division. Sentence C mentions both of these ideas, but the other answer choices do not mention both of them.

31. The correct answer is D. "Latter" means the last thing mentioned. Accommodation is the last function mentioned in the first sentence of paragraph 4.

32. The correct answer is B. "Exemplify" means to give an example. Bottle feeding is given as an example in paragraph 4 because this idea is introduced by using the phrase "for example."

33. The correct answer is D. Paragraph 5 mentions that in this stage "intelligence is demonstrated in the manner in which the infant interacts physically with the world." The words "mobility" and "motor activity" in this paragraph also express the idea of physical movement. Note that "cognitive" means intellectual.

34. The correct answer is A. Paragraph 7 mention that "logical and systematic thought processes appear" during the concrete operational stage. Since these skills appear during the concrete operational stage, they don't exist prior to this time.

35. The correct answer is B. Paragraph 8 states: "adults in many countries have not completed this stage due to the lack of educational opportunities or poverty."

36. The correct answer is B. The author's purpose is clearly stated in the first sentence of the passage: "Jean Piaget is one of the most well-known theorists in child development and educational psychology, and the scholastic community still discusses his principles today."

EXTENDED READING PRACTICE SET 2

1. The correct answer is C. The best title for the passage is "The Changing Face of Tourism." The first sentence of the passage states: "Adventurers, fieldwork assistants, and volunteers are gradually replacing tourists." This sentence introduces the idea of changes to tourism, and these changes are explained in depth in the passage.

2. The correct answer is B. The word "clandestine" has the same meaning as "secret." We know that tourism has become a secret activity because paragraph 1 states that traveling for enjoyment has become a "frowned-upon activity [. . . that] no one will admit to."

3. The correct answer is C. The author does not discuss the reasons why flights became inexpensive. The passage merely states that "the advent of relatively less expensive accommodation and flights has meant that tourism can finally be enjoyed by the majority."

4. The correct answer is A. "Absurd" means ridiculous. The author states that there would be "impediments in attempting to make so many economically-empowered people stop doing something they enjoy" so we know that the author disagrees with the previous assertions in paragraph 5.

5. The correct answer is C. "Emulate" means to imitate. The example in paragraph 8 points out that *Global Adventure* magazine treats charitable expeditions and vacations "as if the two things are one and the same."

6. The correct answer is D. The best place to insert this new sentence is at the end of the passage. The new sentence says that "Our concern should be not with this small number of privileged people, but rather with the majority of travelers." The phrase "this small number of privileged people" refers to the "few affluent and privileged tourists" mentioned at the end of the passage.

7. The correct answer is A. The best paraphrase of the sentence "Whatever benefits or otherwise accrue from tourism, it is not evil, despite what a tiny minority might say" is as follows: "Although the benefits of tourism may be questionable, tourism is not morally wrong, in spite of what a few detractors might believe." The phrase "although the benefits of tourism may be questionable" has the same meaning as "whatever benefits or otherwise accrue from tourism, it is not evil," and the phrase "what a few detractors might believe" has the same meaning as "what a tiny minority might say."

8. The correct answer is A. The phrase "tourist infrastructures" refers to hotels and other physical structures that have been purpose-built for tourists. We know this because the next sentence in paragraph 9 talks about accommodation.

9. The correct answer is D. The words "these notions" refer to the viewpoints that express disdain for tourism. We know this because the previous sentence in the passage expresses the belief that tourism "must be stopped at any price."

10. The correct answer is C. The author mentions "cultural experiences", "expeditions" or "projects" in paragraph 7 of the passage to illustrate how tourism has been re-branded. The last sentence of paragraph 7 states that "re-branding tourism in this way gives freedom to travelers, as well as restrictions."

11. The correct answer is B. Using unconventional types of lodging arrangements characterizes how tourists can be more respectful of their environments. Paragraph 9 states that new tourists "prefer

accommodation arrangements such as cabins or camping. These types of accommodation, they believe, are more respectful of local culture."

12. The correct answer is D. "Affluent" means wealthy. The paragraph also uses the word "privileged," which implies that these tourists have a great deal of money.

13. The correct answer is A. The author expresses regret towards the past effects of tourism on the environment. We can assume that the author feels regret because the last paragraph claims that "all types of tourism should be responsible towards and respectful of environmental and human resources."

14. The correct answer is B. Paragraph 1 does not state that alcohol consumption has risen across many age groups in the last ten years. It merely points out that that there has been an increase in the consumption of alcoholic beverages by a particular group, namely, among the 11-to-15-year-old age group.

15. The correct answer is A. The best definition for the word *tackling* is trying to solve. We can understand this because other parts of the passage point out possible solutions.

16. The correct answer is C. The best explanation of the term health inequalities is that mortality and disease rates are greater for members of poor families. Paragraph 2 emphasizes that "rates of disease and death are far higher in poorer households."

17. The correct answer is D. The word "cynics" is synonymous with the word "doubters." In paragraph 3, we read that the cynics think that the "government's monetary support for poor households will invariably be spent on consumables like candy and potato chips, or other junk food, or worse, on tobacco, alcohol, and even drugs." So, these people do not believe that the government can really help poor families.

18. The correct answer is C. The best place for the new sentence is at the end of paragraph 4. The new sentence states that "giving free school meals to children from lower-income families would be the best and most direct way of improving child nutrition." We know this is the best place because it relates to the "school breakfast and dinner programs" mentioned in the previous sentence in paragraph 4.

19. The correct answer is A. The word "they" refers to countries that have established school breakfasts. The previous sentence in paragraph 5 mentions that "some countries have developed programs for nutritious school breakfasts and dinners."

20. The correct answer is B. The best paraphrase is as follows: "Poor children do not start the day with a good meal and cannot learn well as a result, so it is of the utmost importance for the government to improve child poverty and child nutrition" The phrase "poor children do not start the day with a good meal and cannot learn well as a result" means the same as "disadvantaged children in many areas still do not get a nourishing breakfast and the effectiveness of their education is jeopardized as a result." The phrase "so it is of the utmost importance for the government to improve child poverty and child nutrition" means the same thing as "there remains a clear need for the authorities to address nutrition as one of the worst symptoms of child poverty."

21. The correct answer is D. The author discusses smoking in paragraph 6 in order to expand on another aspect of poor health in children. We know this because the first sentence of paragraph 6 points out that "smoking also greatly damages the health of children and increases childhood mortality rates."

22. The correct answer is C. The main reason for the government's increase in the cigarette tax was to attempt to deter smoking, particularly by poor parents. Paragraph 6 states that the cigarette tax "has left poor parents who smoke worse off." So, we can assume that these poor parents have continued to smoke, and are now paying more for their smoking habit, thereby having less to spend on nutritious food.

23. The correct answer is B. The word "palatable" means tasty. We can understand this because paragraph 7 stresses that these drinks are sweet.

24. The correct answer is A. Based on paragraph 7, we can infer that the government is reluctant to criticize the practices of big businesses because it is loath to lose the monetary support that large beverage companies have to offer. "Loath" means "unwilling or reluctant."

25. The correct answer is D. The relationship between the goals of improved opportunities for children and the problems of child poverty and ill health is best described as follows: The achievement of the goal of the reduction of child poverty would improve child health and increase the opportunities of children to some extent, but it would not entirely eradicate the problem. Paragraph 8 states that "while these goals are related, it would be foolish to believe that the reduction of child poverty would automatically improve children's nutrition and reduce their smoking and drinking."

26. The correct answer is C. The author's main purpose in the passage is to enumerate the reasons for health inequalities, particularly in children, and to allude to some possible courses of action. Paragraph 4 mentions the solution of school breakfast and dinner programs. Paragraph 5 asserts that the "authorities [need] to address nutrition as one of the worst symptoms of child poverty." Paragraph 6 claims that more government funds should be allocated to preventing cigarette sales to children. Finally, the last paragraph proposes "the allocation of governmental funds to nutrition and effective education."

27. The correct answer is C. The word "catalyst" in this passage is closest in meaning to "reason." We know that immigration is the reason because paragraph 1 states that the population has risen because immigration has increased.

28. The correct answer is B. The words "this steady influx" refer to the constant increase in people coming to the country for the first time. The previous paragraph describes how net inward migration increased during the study.

29. The correct answer is A. The most notable change to the population in the last one hundred years was the three-fold increase in the size of the population. Paragraph 3 clarifies that "notably, the population tripled from almost 76 million at the beginning of the twentieth century to nearly 281 million at the start of the twenty-first century."

30. The correct answer is B. The best place for the new sentence is near the start of paragraph 3, which discusses changes to average household size.

31. The correct answer is D. The word "outstrip" in this passage is closest in meaning to the word "exceed." The paragraph states that "the population density of the Northeast . . . has always been high."

32. The correct answer is A. The author mentions the changes to the populations of Florida and Arizona to point out that new residents are continually moving to these states." Paragraph 3 mentions that "Florida and Arizona had the fastest-growing populations during the period of the study."

33. The correct answer is C. The phrase "lion's share of" is closest in meaning to "majority of." The sentence is talking about an increase in consumer credit, so we can surmise that credit cards are the primary cause for this phenomenon.

34. The correct answer is B. A possible interpretation is that the divorce rate went down because fewer people got married during the period of the study. The author's use of the word "concurrent" emphasizes that the decline in the marriage rate and the decrease in the divorce rate occurred at the same time.

35. The correct answer is D. The most notable demographic shift when comparing geographic areas was that many people moved from the Northeast and Midwest to live in the South or West. Paragraph 4

emphasizes that "until 1970 the majority of households were living in the Northeast and Midwest, but since 1980 the majority was in the South and West."

36. The correct answer is C. We can infer that women are more likely to live alone after losing a life partner than men are. Paragraph 4 points out that "female householders have increased as a proportion of all householders, and older females were far more likely to live alone than were men." We can infer that one of the primary reasons for living alone is losing one's life partner through death or breakup.

37. The correct answer is A. Paragraphs 1 and 2 talk about how the population has increased as a result of immigration. Paragraphs 3 and 4 discuss notable changes in the concentration of the population in certain states and geographic regions, and paragraph 5 describes the way in which the distribution of income has become increasingly skewed in favor of the rich.

CITATION, REFERENCING, AND PLAGIARISM EXERCISES

1. The correct answer is A. Answer A is correct because it uses the quotation without changing or adding any words, it places the speaker's exact words in quotation marks, and it attributes the quotation to the person who said it. Answers B and C have changed the words of the quotations, and answer D draws a conclusion that is not directly supported by the quotation.

2. The correct answer is C. Secondary sources provide commentary on primary sources. Refer back to the referencing and citation section of the study guide if you are still unsure about the difference between primary and secondary sources.

3. The correct answer is A. The indication of a volume and issue number ["125(3)"] indicates that a scholarly journal is being cited.

4. The correct answer is D. Answers A, B, and C address the new federal regulation or previous federal regulations on the subject of carbon emissions. Answer D is on state laws, not federal regulations, so it is not directly relevant.

5. The correct answer is B. Answers A and C are secondary sources on the subject of climate change. Answer D is a primary source on pollution, rather than climate change itself, so it is slightly off the point. A scientific study is one type of primary source, so answer B is the correct response.

6. The correct answer is A. Remember that a primary source provides statistical or documentary evidence.

7. The correct answer is C. The reading list will show other books and articles on the subject that you are researching, so you can use it to identify further sources that you can read on your subject.

8. The correct answer is D. We know that a book is being cited because the title is given in italics. In addition, a year is given, rather than a specific date, which identifies the source as a book.

9. The correct answer is C. Answer A provides a source that is much too general. Answers B and D would be biased towards the local level, rather than focusing on the entire state. Answer C is the only response that focuses on the state-wide level.

10. The correct answer is B. This is a case of plagiarism because it uses the exact words of the quotation, without placing quotation marks around them, as has been correctly done in answers A and D. Answer C is not plagiarism because it provides an accurate paraphrase of the ideas contained in the quotation.

GRAMMAR REVIEW EXERCISES – SET 1

1. C
2. B
3. A
4. C
5. D
6. A
7. B
8. A
9. C
10. A
11. C
12. B
13. D
14. C
15. B

GRAMMAR REVIEW EXERCISES – SET 2

1. D
2. D
3. C
4. D
5. C
6. D
7. B
8. C
9. C
10. A

11. B

12. A

13. D

14. C

15. A

GRAMMAR REVIEW EXERCISES – SET 3

1. A

2. C

3. A

4. B

5. A

6. A

7. C

8. B

9. C

10. A

11. A

12. D

13. B

14. B

15. B

GRAMMAR REVIEW EXERCISES – SET 4

1. The correct answer is A. We need the noncomparative adjective "anywhere" because we are not making a comparison in the sentence.

2. The correct answer is B. We are indicating that the job is nearly done, so we need the adverb of degree "almost."

3. The correct answer is D. The emphatic form is needed here because we are contrasting the accident to the carefulness. The action is in the past, so the correct answer is "did have."

4. The correct answer is B. We need the accusative form "me" because of the preposition "between."

5. The correct answer is C. The plural form is required because of the plural noun "people" earlier in the sentence.

6. The correct answer is A. The relative pronoun "whose" is correct since the name belongs to the student.

7. The correct answer is B. We are describing a strong obligation or expectation in the recent past, so we need to use "should have" in this sentence.

8. The correct answer is A. We know that the superlative form is needed in this sentence because of the article "the."

9. The correct answer is D. The connective "in spite of that" is needed because of the word "but," which shows a contrast is going to be made. The other answer choices are not grammatically correct.

10. The correct answer is D. This is a form of the third conditional, so the inverted form of the past perfect "had I had" is the correct answer.

11. The correct answer is A. The verb "decide" takes the infinitive, so "to attend" is the correct answer. Notice that the verb "attend" in this context is a transitive verb, so we don't need a preposition.

12. The correct answer is C. "Get away with" means to escape the consequences of your actions.

13. The correct answer is B. The verb "be" is needed after the modal verb "can." We are describing an action, so we need the adverb "easily" rather than the adjective "easy."

14. The correct answer is C. "Not a word" is a negative adverbial clause, so we need to invert the auxiliary verb "did" to get the correct answer "did he say."

15. The correct answer is B. The word "all" needs the preposition "of." The definite article is needed because we are describing something specific, i.e., the new merchandise.

16. The correct answer is A. The passive form of the perfect infinitive is required since we have the verb "are believed."

17. The correct answer is B. The noun phrase "the beginning" needs to be preceded by the preposition "at."

18. The correct answer is A. We need the third conditional form in this sentence since we have the past perfect "hadn't eaten." Remember that you can use "might" instead of "would" in the third conditional.

19. The correct answer is B. We need the singular demonstrative pronoun "this" because the noun "book" is singular.

20. The correct answer is C. The need the plural form "others" because of the word "many."

GRAMMAR REVIEW EXERCISES – SET 5

1. The correct answer is C. We have the negative adverbial "very rarely" so we need to invert the auxiliary verb for the correct form "does she appear."

2. The correct answer is A. The relative pronoun "that" is correct since there is a clause after the gap.

3. The correct answer is C. "Size up" is a phrasal verb that means to measure or estimate something.

4. The correct answer is A. The verb "hope" takes the infinitive form, so the correct answer is "to go." The perfect infinitive in answer choice D is incorrect because we are speaking about an action in the future.

5. The correct answer is C. "No sooner" is a negative adverbial, so we need to invert the auxiliary verb for the correct form "had we arrived."

6. The correct answer is D. The verb "recover" takes the preposition "from."

7. The correct answer is B. We have the third conditional here because of the verb "wouldn't have gotten." So, the past perfect "had she been" is needed in the second part of the sentence. We have not used the word "if," so we need to put the auxiliary verb "had" before the pronoun "she."

8. The correct answer is B. We can omit the use of a relative pronoun in this sentence. The correct word order is subject + verb + adverb, so we need the answer "I saw last week."

9. The correct answer is D. We need the bare form of the passive infinitive "be invited" because of the use of the verb "requested" and the relative pronoun "that."

10. The correct answer is C. The superlative form (without "the") is needed here because of the phrase "one of" earlier in the sentence.

11. The correct answer is A. We are talking about a strong obligation in the recent past, so the correct answer is "you should have filled."

12. The correct answer is B. We are making a comparison in this sentence to McDonald's, so we need the comparative adverb of place "somewhere else."

13. The correct answer is D. We need "most" because we are describing the majority of students.

14. The correct answer is A. The verb "deny" takes the gerund form, so "stealing" is the correct answer.

15. The correct answer is C. "Put up with" is a phrasal verb that means to tolerate something or someone.

16. The correct answer is B. We need the phrase linker "because of" since the gap is followed by a phrase, rather than a clause.

17. The correct answer is A. The word "other" is used to modify the plural noun "hobbies."

18. The correct answer is B. The emphatic form "do need" is correct since we are emphasizing a generalization or habit.

19. The correct answer is B. The active form of the perfect infinitive form "to have worked" is correct since the sentence is talking about an action in the recent past.

20. The correct answer is A. The pronouns "you and he" are needed he since they form the subject of this clause in the sentence.

SENTENCE CORRECTION AND REVISION PRACTICE SET 1

1. The correct answer is D. The phrase *Although only sixteen years old* modifies the pronoun "she." Therefore, "she" needs to come after this phrase.

2. The correct answer is A. This question is an example of the inverted sentence structure. When a sentence begins with a negative phrase [no sooner, not only, never, etc.], the present perfect tense [have + past participle] must be used. In addition, the auxiliary verb "have" must be placed in front of the grammatical subject of the sentence [I].

3. The correct answer is B. This question is about "parallelism." In order to follow the grammatical rules of parallelism, you must be sure that all of the items you give in a list are of the same part of speech. So, all of the items must be nouns or verbs, for example. In other words, you should not use both nouns and verbs in a list. Answer B has all nouns, but the other answer choices have some nouns and some verbs.

4. The correct answer is D. This question is about the use of punctuation. "However, the noise next door made it impossible" is a complete sentence. It has a grammatical subject [the noise] and a verb [made]. "However" must be preceded by a period, and the new sentence must begin with a capital letter. In addition, "however" is a sentence linker. So, "however" must be followed by a comma.

5. The correct answer is A. The words "which would be spacious enough to transport her equipment" form a restrictive modifier. A restrictive modifier is a clause or phrase that provides essential information about a noun in the sentence. In other words, we would not know exactly what kind of new car she wanted without the clause "which would be spacious enough to transport her equipment." Restrictive modifiers should not be preceded by a comma.

6. The correct answer is C. The prepositional phrase "Near a small river at the bottom of the canyon" describes the location of the people when they made their discovery. So, the prepositional phrase must be followed by "we." Since the prepositional phrase is at the beginning of the sentence, the complete phrase needs to be followed with a comma. Note that you need to put in only one comma at the end of such prepositional phrases.

7. The correct answer is B. This question tests your knowledge of "who" and "whom." Remember to use "who" when the person you are talking about is doing the action, but to use "whom" when the person is receiving an action. In this sentence, the candidate is receiving the action of being selected. So, the question should begin with "whom." The auxiliary verb "did" needs to come directly after "whom" to have the correct word order for this type of question.

8. The correct answer is A. The phrase "Always and Forever" is an example of a restrictive modifier. As mentioned in question number 5, restrictive modifiers are clauses or phrases that provide essential information in order to identify the subject. In other words, without the phrase "Always and Forever" in this sentence, we would not know exactly which song they played at their wedding. So, the phrase conveys essential information. Note that restrictive modifiers should not be preceded by a comma.

9. The correct answer is B. In this sentence, the word "as" functions as a subordinating conjunction. Commas should not be placed before subordinating conjunctions. Other examples of subordinating conjunctions are "because" and "since."

10. The correct answer is C. If you are talking about yourself in an imaginary situation, you need to use *were* instead of *was*. This is known as the subjunctive mood. In the other half of the sentence, you need to use the verb "would" when you are describing an imaginary situation.

11. The correct answer is B. The new sentence would be constructed as follows: Even though she worked all night, she still did not finish the project. Sentences that begin with "even though" are used to introduce an unexpected result to a situation. Remember that "even though" is used to join subordinate clauses to sentences. Subordinate clauses contain a grammatical subject (she) and a verb (worked).

12. The correct answer is C. The new sentence would be constructed as follows: Despite snow showers being common in the north during the winter, precipitation is unlikely tomorrow. "Despite" takes a noun phrase, not a clause. In other words, the part of the sentence that contains "despite" should not include a verb. "Despite" should also not be followed directly by "of." In this example, the word "being" functions as an adjectival phrase, not a verb.

13. The correct answer is D. The new sentence would be constructed as follows: Because it is warm all year round, Florida has many out-of-state visitors during December and January. "Because" is a subordinator. In other words, the part of the sentence that includes "because" also needs to include a verb. Answer D contains a verb [is], but the other answers do not have verbs.

14. The correct answer is A. The new sentence is: Just as Tom is highly intelligent, so too is his younger brother. Comparative sentences that begin with "just as" need to include "so too" in the other part of the sentence.

15. The correct answer is B. The new sentence is formed as follows: After Mary had arrived at the party, I decided to go home. Clauses that begin with "After" normally need to contain the past perfect tense. The past perfect tense is formed with "had" plus the past participle, which is "arrived" in this sentence.

16. The correct answer is C. "Provided" is used in sentences in the same way as "if." So, in the above sentence, we can replace "if" with "provided." In addition, the end of the original sentence is moved to the beginning of the new sentence. Be sure you put a comma after the "if" clause once you have changed the order of the clauses in the sentence. The new sentence is: Provided you work hard, you will succeed at college.

17. The correct answer is B. The phrase "kind and patient" modifies the word "teacher." Therefore, your new sentence will be: Kind and patient, she is a good teacher.

18. The correct answer is A. The new sentence is constructed as follows: Besides being rude, she is also stingy. In sentences like this, you can just replace the phrase "apart from" with the word "besides."

19. The correct answer is D. The new sentence is: Because of the student's insolence, the teacher became upset. Remember that "because" is a subordinator. So, "because" needs to be followed by a verb. On the other hand, "because of" is a phrase linker. So, the part of the sentence that contains "because of" needs to be followed by a noun phrase. "The student's insolence" is a noun phrase.

20. The correct answer is C. The new sentence is: Increasing numbers of teenagers are developing type II diabetes. The word "increasing" needs to be followed by "numbers" or "amounts."

SENTENCE CORRECTION AND REVISION PRACTICE SET 2

1. The correct answer is C. This question is about the use of punctuation. "However, they were out of reach" is a complete sentence. It has a grammatical subject [they] and a verb [were]. "However" must be preceded by a period, and the new sentence must begin with a capital letter. Compare the placement of "however" and the punctuation in these sentences: The child tried to grab the cookies from the shelf. They were, however, out of reach. When you use the word "however" in the middle of a sentence, "however" must be preceded by a comma and also followed by a comma.

2. The correct answer is C. "Covered in chocolate frosting" is a past participle phrase that describes the cake. In other words, the hostess is not covered in chocolate frosting. Therefore, the words "the cake" must follow the past participle phrase. Remember: past participle phrases are those that begin with verbs that end in -ed (in the case of regular verbs). You need to be sure that you have the participle phrase next to the noun that the phrase is describing.

3. The correct answer is A. This is another question about "parallelism." Be sure that all of the items you give in a list are of the same part of speech, nouns or verbs, for example. In other words, you should not use both nouns and verbs in a list. In addition, all of the verbs you use must be in the same tense. In answer A, both verbs are in the "to" form. The other answers combine -ing and -ed verbs.

4. The correct answer is A. The words "one which he could use to gaze at the stars" form a dependent relative clause. A relative clause often contains "that" or "which." A dependent clause cannot stand alone as a complete sentence. Since it is a non-restrictive (non-essential) relative clause, it must be preceded by a comma.

5. The correct answer is C. This question is another example of the inverted sentence structure. When a sentence begins with a negative phrase [no sooner, not only, never, etc.], the past perfect tense [had + past participle] must be used. In addition, the auxiliary verb "had" must be placed in front of the grammatical subject of the sentence [I].

6. The correct answer is B. This question tests your knowledge of conditional sentence structures. Conditional sentences often begin with the word *if*. Conditional sentences may express generalizations, as in this sentence. Therefore, the simple present tense (go) is used in the "If" clause, and the simple present (try) is also used in the main part of the sentence. The two parts of a conditional sentence must be separated by a comma.

7. The correct answer is B. Punctuation should be enclosed within the final quotation mark when giving dialogue. The word *said* shows that the comma needed.

8. The correct answer is D. The phrase "is known as" must be preceded with a noun phrase. "The experience of confusion about one's own identity" is a noun phrase. "Is known as" must not be preceded with a verb. No comma or pronoun (e.g., this, it) is needed.

9. The correct answer is C. "Upset from receiving the bad news" modifies or describes Mary. So, this phrase must be followed with a comma. No additional commas are needed.

10. The correct answer is D. "Dilapidated and disheveled" is a past participle phrase that describes the house. Therefore, "Dilapidated and disheveled" must be followed by a comma.

11. The correct answer is B. The new sentence is: She was excited because she finally got that new car, which she had wanted for so long. We need to put a comma after "car" because "which" forms a non-restrictive relative clause. Remember that non-restrictive relative clauses convey non-essential information and that non-restrictive relative clauses must be preceded by a comma. The phrase "which

she had wanted for so long" is non-essential because we have already identified the car earlier in the sentence with the phrase "that car."

12. The correct answer is C. The new sentence is: Unlike my physics tests, my math test will be easy to pass. The phrase "Unlike my physics test" is an adjectival phrase that modifies (or makes a comparison with) "my math test." Therefore, "my math test" must come directly after the comma.

13. The correct answer is D. The new sentence is: Having felt ill for days, she eventually came down with the flu. Phrases that begin with verbs in the -ing form are known as present participle phrases. In the new sentence, the present participle phrase "Having felt ill for days" modifies "she." Therefore, "she" must come directly after the comma.

14. The correct answer is A. The new sentence would be constructed as follows: She is not able to come to Hawaii with us because she cannot afford it. Remember that "because" is used to join subordinate clauses to sentences. Subordinate clauses contain a grammatical subject (she) and a verb (cannot afford), but they cannot stand alone as complete sentences.

15. The correct answer is C. The new sentence is: The game began after the referee blew his whistle. The word "after" begins the subordinate clause in the second part of the new sentence. Since the first part of the new sentence contains the past tense (began), the second part of the new sentence should also contain the past tense (blew). The words "the referee" form the grammatical subject of the subordinate clause.

16. The correct answer is B. The new sentence is: Whereas Thomas studied extensively for his final exams, Mary did not. The sentence begins with "whereas," a word which introduces a contrast or contradiction. Negative forms of the verb must be used in the second part of the sentence if the sentence begins with "whereas." So, the negative form of the verb "did not" must be used in the second part of this sentence. Therefore, answers C and D are incorrect. Answer A is incorrect because "whereas" already conveys the idea of contrast, so "unlike" would repeat the idea of contrast.

17. The correct answer is D. The new sentence is: Unless he receives approval from his superiors, he will not get the promotion. Negative forms of the verb must be used in the second part of the sentence if the sentence begins with "unless." So, the negative form of the verb "will not get" must be used in the second part of this sentence.

18. The correct answer is A. The new sentence would be constructed as follows: Although she gave her best effort, Barbara failed to complete the project on time. The word "although" is another subordinating conjunction used to join subordinate clauses to sentences.

19. The correct answer is D. The new sentence is: Sarah, whose father was a foreign diplomat, has lived in many locations around the world. The comma after "Sarah" indicates that a relative clause (e.g., whose) must be used. "Whose" is used to describe something that belongs to a person. In this sentence, we could say that Sarah's father "belongs" to her. So, the word "father" must come after "whose." Remember that relative clauses include the following words: who, which, that, whom, whose.

20. The correct answer is B. The new sentence is: Because of its high academic standards, Harvard attracts the best and brightest students each year. The phrase linker "because of" is used to join a noun phrase to a sentence. Remember that noun phrases do not contain verbs and cannot stand alone as complete sentences. Answers A and D are adjectival phrases, and answer C contains a verb. Answer B is the only choice that contains a noun phrase.

SENTENCE CORRECTION AND REVISION PRACTICE SET 3

1. The correct answer is D. The phrase *while at the mall* modifies the pronoun "I." So, "I" needs to come after this phrase.

2. The correct answer is C. When a compound sentence contains the word "just" to describe an action that has recently been completed, the past perfect tense [had + past participle] should be used in the part of the sentence containing the word "just."

3. The correct answer is D. This question is about the use of punctuation. "Then our plans changed" is an independent clause. It has a grammatical subject [our plans] and a verb [changed]. According to traditional rules of grammar, "and" is a coordinating conjunction, used to combine phrases or clauses within a sentence. Since "and" is a conjunction, we should avoid beginning sentences with "and." So, the word "and" should be included within a single sentence and preceded by a comma.

4. The correct answer is C. This question is about gerunds, also known as -ing words or verbal nouns. Note that the -ing form is usually used when discussing activities or hobbies.

5. The correct answer is A. Exasperated is a past participle phrase that describes Bill. So, the sentence is correct as it is written.

6. The correct answer is A. The words "that would accommodate all of his oversized furniture" form a dependent relative clause. A dependent relative clause containing "that" is not preceded by a comma.

7. The correct answer is C. Punctuation should be enclosed within the final quotation mark when giving dialogue. The word *exclaimed* shows that the exclamation point is needed.

8. The correct answer is B. The phrase "in spite of" must be followed by a noun or noun phrase. "In spite of" should not be followed by a clause. The -ing form "studying" is used as a gerund (a verbal noun) in this sentence.

9. The correct answer is D. This question tests your knowledge of the comparative and superlative forms. Use the comparative form (-er) when comparing two things. If you are comparing more than two things, you must use the superlative form (-est).

10. The correct answer is C. This question tests your knowledge of conditional sentence structures. Conditional sentences often begin with the word *if*. Conditional sentences may address hypothetical or imaginary situations. This sentence mentions a hypothetical situation. Therefore, the simple present tense (steal) is used in the "If" clause, and the modal verb (could) is used in the main part of the sentence. The two parts of conditional sentences beginning with "if" must be separated by a comma.

11. The correct answer is B. The new sentence is: Once they had checked the extent of the man's injuries, the paramedics put him into the ambulance. Clauses that begin with "once" need to contain the past perfect tense. The past perfect tense is formed with "had" plus the past participle, which is "checked" in this sentence.

12. The correct answer is A. The new sentence is: I was embarrassed when the professor praised my exam score in front of the other students. The word "when" forms a subordinate clause in the second part of the new sentence. Since the first part of the new sentence contains the past tense (was), the second part of the new sentence also contains the past tense (praised). The words "the professor" form the grammatical subject of the subordinate clause. Therefore, the pronoun "he" is not needed.

13. The correct answer is A. The new sentence is: Like Minnesota, Wisconsin gets extremely cold in the winter. The phrase "like Minnesota" is an adjectival phrase that modifies the noun "Wisconsin." Therefore, "Wisconsin" must come directly after the comma.

14. The correct answer is C. The new sentence is: The Grand Canyon is a popular tourist destination because it is rich in natural beauty and abundant in wildlife. The word "because" is used to join a subordinate clause to a sentence. Remember that clauses are distinct from phrases because clauses contain both a grammatical subject and a verb. "It" is the grammatical subject in the subordinate clause of the new sentence and "is" is the verb.

15. The correct answer is D. The new sentence is: My sister, who was ill, stayed home from school. The comma after "my sister" indicates that a relative clause must be used. Remember that relative clauses can include the following words: who, which, that, whom, whose.

16. The correct answer is C. The new sentence is: In the event of rain tomorrow, the picnic will have to be canceled. The phrase "in the event of" should be followed by a noun or noun phrase. In addition, the verb must be changed to the passive from, using the verb "be."

17. The correct answer is B. The new sentence would be constructed as follows: The team was so disappointed when it lost the championship game. The grammatical construction is similar to question 12 above.

18. The correct answer is A. The new sentence would be constructed as follows: Although he trained for years, he was not selected for the Olympics. Sentences that begin with "although" introduce an unexpected result to a situation.

19. The correct answer is C. The new sentence is: Watching television, he fell asleep and began snoring. Phrases that begin with verbs in the -ing form are known as present participle phrases. In the new sentence, the present participle phrase "watching television" modifies "he." Therefore, "he" must come directly after the comma.

20. The correct answer is D. The new sentence is as follows: Suffering from homesickness is common among students who study at colleges in other states. In the new sentence, the -ing form (suffering) is used as a gerund. So, "suffering from homesickness" is the grammatical subject of the new sentence. The grammatical subject is followed by a verb (is) and an adjective (common). Note that "commonality" is a noun.

SENTENCE CORRECTION AND REVISION PRACTICE SET 4

1. You should select: No error. The sentence contains no errors in grammar or usage.

2. You should select: their. The antecedent is "chicory," which is singular. So, the pronoun "it" should be used before the grammatical subject, rather than "their."

3. You should select: compositions are. The grammatical subject of this clause is the word "what." Therefore, we need to use the singular form of the verb (is).

4. You should select: organ's. The plural form "organs" is needed. The possessive form "organ's" is incorrect because there is no corresponding noun for the possessive.

5. You should select: No error. The sentence contains no errors in grammar or usage.

6. You should select: to. The verb "differentiate" takes the preposition "from", not "to."

7. You should select: no. The sentence contains a double negative since the word "cannot" is used earlier in the sentence. So, "any" should be used here.

8. You should select: roman. Roman is a proper noun, so it needs to be capitalized.

9. You should select: among. Only two counties are mentioned, so the word "between" is needed.

10. You should select: the comma. The comma is incorrect since it unnaturally divides the subject and verb of the clause.

11. You should select: explorer's. The second part of the sentence is describing more than one explorer since the word "them" is used later in the sentence. Therefore, the plural possessive is needed (explorers').

12. You should select: die. The sentence is written in the past simple tense, so the verb form "died" should be used.

13. You should select: effected. The verb form (affected) is required since the sentence is talking about the changes that were a result of the Women's Rights Movement.

14. You should select: constitute. The subject of the sentence is "migration" so the singular verb form (constitutes) should be used.

15. You should select: and. We can see the use of "not only" earlier in the sentence, so we need "but also," instead of "and also"

16. You should select: that. The subject of this part of the sentence is the plural "settlers," so the plural pronoun "those" is needed, rather than "that."

17. You should select: having played. The perfect infinitive verb form "to have played" is needed because we are talking about a topic that has current relevance. We know that the topic is under current discussion because of the word "arguably" earlier in the sentence.

18. You should select: having. The subject of the sentence is "system," so the present simple verb form "has" is needed.

19. You should select: principle. You should use the word "principal" as an adjective in this sentence, rather than the noun form "principle."

20. The correct answer is C. The antecedent is "Siluriformes," which is plural. However, "its mouth" is singular. Therefore, the plural pronoun "their" and the plural noun "mouths" need to be used in order to correct the error.

21. The correct answer is C. Because of the placement of modifying phrase at the beginning, the sentence as written suggests that the tire is driving the car. The pronoun "I" needs to be placed after the introductory phrase since the speaker was driving the car. Remember to place the modifying phrase directly before the noun that it modifies.

22. The correct answer is B. The sentence contains a lack of parallel structure ("for having worked [. . .], retaining [. . .], and the special"). Answer B correctly uses the –ing form in all three verbs in order to correct the error.

23. The correct answer is D. The sentence as written is an example of a run-on sentence. The word "but" correctly subordinates the second part of the sentence.

24. The correct answer is E. The sentence has an error in parallelism. All of the hobbies should be stated in the –ing form, so E is the correct response.

25. The correct answer is D. This sentence also has an error in parallelism. All of actions should be stated in the –ed (past simple) form, so D is the correct response.

26. The correct answer is C. The sentence has an error in parallel construction, since it uses the –ed form of the verb ("disregarded") and the –ing form of the verb ("rebelling") in the same part of the sentence. There is no problem with the relative pronoun usage ("who") in the original sentence. Answer C correctly uses "who" and constructs both verbs in the –ed form

27. The correct answer is E. The sentence as written is a fragment. Replacing the –ing form "having" with the past simple tense ("avoided") completes the sentence correctly since the action described in the sentence occurred in the past.

28. The correct answer is C. The sentence as written incorrectly implies that the rocks, rather than the minerals, form the crystals. Response C corrects this error by using the verb "to form."

29. The correct answer is B. The highlighted part of the sentence is missing a relative pronoun ("that"). In addition, a comma needs to be placed before the grammatical subject of the sentence ("the congressman").

30. The correct answer is C. Since the pronoun "you" is used in the second part of the sentence, the same pronoun is also required in the first part of the sentence. The sentence is describing a generalization, so the present simple tense ("message") is needed, rather than the continuous form ("messaging").

SENTENCE CORRECTION AND REVISION PRACTICE SET 5

1. You should select: the comma. Remember that a comma should not be used before "that" when forming relative clauses.

2. You should select: themselves. The subject of this clause is "any substance," so the singular form of the pronoun (itself) should be used.

3. You should select: moorish. Moorish is a proper adjective, so it needs to be capitalized.

4. You should select: no error. The sentence contains no errors in grammar or usage.

5. You should select: spanned. The bridge spans the bay, so the passive verb form (is spanned) is needed in this sentence.

6. You should select: used. The sentence is describing a scientific principle, so the present simple tense (use) is required.

7. You should select: no comma. A comma should be placed after the adverb "theoretically" since this adverb is placed at the beginning of the sentence.

8. You should select: the semicolon. The word "however" forms a new sentence because it is capitalized, so a period needs to be used here, instead of the semicolon.

9. You should select: no error. The sentence contains no errors in grammar or usage.

10. You should select: it evaluates. The subject of the sentence is "disciplines," which is plural, so the clause should use the plural form "they evaluate."

11. You should select: no error. The sentence contains no errors in grammar or usage.

12. You should select: having been assassinated. The perfect passive infinitive verb form "to have been assassinated" is needed because the word "indisputably" earlier in the sentence shows that this topic is still of current interest.

13. You should select: with. The word "impact" takes the preposition "on."

14. You should select: going. The simple present form of the verb "go" needs to be used in this sentence in order to form a parallel structure with the simple present form of the verb "be" in the "not only" clause of the sentence.

15. You should select: that make. The subject of the clause is "sequence", which is singular, so the verb "makes" is needed.

16. You should select: no error. The sentence contains no errors in grammar or usage.

17. You should select: no comma. A comma is needed before the word "who" because this part of the sentence forms a non-defining relative clause. In other words, the name of the king is provided, so this part of the sentence just gives additional information.

18. You should select: his. The subject of the clause is "work," which is singular, so the pronoun "its" should be used.

19. You should select: Northeast. The adjective should not be capitalized since it is not a proper adjective.

20. correct answer is B. The subject of the sentence is "colleges," so the plural form of the pronoun ("their") needs to be used. The Antebellum Period is in the past, so the past simple tense ("included") is the correct verb form.

21. The correct answer is E. The base form of the verb "see" is used in the second part of the sentence, so the verb "to overcome" is needed in order to create the correct parallel structure between the verb forms.

22. The correct answer is E. The subject of the sentence is singular ("a country's commerce"). Accordingly, the singular pronoun ("its") is correct. In addition, the infinitive verb form ("to grow") is required since the preceding verb forms are in the infinitive form ("to export [. . .] to invest").

23. The correct answer is C. The sentence describes an action that was completed in the past, so the past simple form ("promoted") is correct.

24. The correct answer is D. The sentence as written has a misplaced modifying phrase and thereby suggests that the embassy contains the confidential information. The letter, rather than the embassy, contains the confidential information, so the modifying phrase ("containing confidential information") needs to be placed directly after the noun to which it relates ("the letter").

25. The correct answer is C. All of the verb forms need to be in the –ing form in order to create the correct parallel structure.

26. The correct answer is A. The sentence is correct as written since both verbs in the modifying phrase are in the –ing form ("drafting [. . .] and serving").

27. The correct answer is D. The sentence as written suggests that the plant is popular simply because it is indigenous to the northern hemisphere. By beginning the sentence with "since," the correct emphasis is placed on the climbing aspect of honeysuckle, which is what makes the plant popular in patios and gardens.

28. The correct answer is B. The introductory phrase "overworked and underpaid" describes the grammatical subject "many employees." Therefore, a comma needs to be used after the word "underpaid."

29. The correct answer is E. The phrase "With its sub-zero temperatures and frozen landscape" describes Siberia, so the word "Siberia" needs to be placed after the comma.

30. The correct answer is D. As written, the sentence contains a fragment ("When air rises and condenses into precipitation"). Answer D is the only response that corrects the fragment without improperly using the demonstrative pronoun "this."

VOCABULARY EXERCISES

1. The correct answer is D. *Acquiesce* means to comply to someone's wishes or to accommodate their requests.

2. The correct answer is C. *Patent* means obvious or apparent. It is most similar in meaning to the word *visible*.

3. The correct answer is A. Lenient means that you are forgiving or forbearing of another person's behavior, so it is closest in meaning to *easy-going*.

4. The correct answer is A. *Propitiate* means placate or pacify, so it is closest in meaning to the word *appease*.

5. The correct answer is C. *Opprobrious* means malicious or damaging.

6. The correct answer is A. The phrase *engulfed in* is the best grammatically and colloquially, since it is the phrase that is most often used to describe fires.

7. The correct answer is B. *Contemplate* means to mull over or think about something deeply.

8. The correct answer is D. To be galvanized into action means that something makes you determined and resolute about achieving a goal.

9. The correct answer is A. The word *temperamental* refers to someone who is irritable or easily upset.

10. The correct answer is B. A precedent creates a criterion or paradigm. So, it is closest to the word *exemplar*.

11. The correct answer is A. *Commend* means to credit someone with an achievement or to acclaim or praise an achievement.

12. The correct answer is C. The word *ostensibly* has the same meaning as the words *evidently* or *supposedly.*

13. The correct answer is C. The word *advocate,* when used as a noun, refers to someone who promotes or supports a certain issue. *Judge* is too formal in this instance, and *arbiter* refers to someone who arbitrates or acts as a go-between.

14. The correct answer is B. *Laud* means to praise or honor someone for his or her actions.

15. The correct answer is C. The word *dubious* refers to something that is unreliable or questionable in quality.

16. The correct answer is A. *Perturb* means to disturb or annoy someone.

17. The correct answer is A. *Alacrity* means enthusiasm or readiness, especially when approaching a task that needs to be done.

18. The correct answer is D. *Dormant* refers to something that is inactive or abeyant.

19. The correct answer is D. *Ingenious* refers to an idea that is original and clever.

20. The correct answer is B. *Toxic* means poisonous or harmful to the health.

21. The correct answer is C. The other answers do not make sense grammatically or lexically.

22. The correct answer is A. Extenuating circumstances are those that lessen, mitigate, or excuse the seriousness of a situation.

23. The correct answer is C. The word *nebulous* refers to something that is unclear.

24. The correct answer is D. *Servility* means enslavement, servitude, or subjugation.

25. The correct answer is C. *Indispensable* means essential, crucial, or fundamental. It is the opposite of *superfluous.*

26. The correct answer is B. A sycophant is someone who uses flattery or servility to win another person's favor.

27. The correct answer is C. *Upheaval* means disturbance, disruption, or disorder.

28. The correct answer is B. *Exonerate* means to be pardoned or acquitted of a charge.

29. The correct answer is A. Since most people don't wear this kind of clothing, it would be considered unconventional.

30. The correct answer is C. *Acrimony* means discord or animosity.

31. The correct answer is A. *Intricate* in this context means detailed or complex.

32. The correct answer is C. *Clemency* means mercy or compassion.

33. The correct answer is A. *Abridge* means to shorten or condense a piece of writing.

34. The correct answer is A. *Stalwart* means dependable and fearless.

35. The correct answer is B. *Entice* means to attract or beguile someone.

36. The correct answer is B. *Earnest* means sincere or heartfelt.

37. The correct answer is B. *Adept* means extremely capable or proficient.

38. The correct answer is A. If someone is indignant about something, he or she is annoyed and resentful.

39. The correct answer is D. A furor over something means that there is a commotion or outburst.

40. The correct answer is D. *Jovial* means having a cheerful or jolly disposition.

ESSAY CORRECTION EXERCISES

Antarctica Essay

1. A
2. C
3. D
4. C
5. A
6. B
7. B
8. B
9. D
10. C
11. A
12. B
13. C
14. B
15. B
16. E
17. C
18. B
19. D
20. E

Population Age-Sex Structure Essay

1. D
2. B
3. A
4. E
5. B
6. C
7. D
8. B
9. C
10. B
11. C
12. B
13. D
14. C
15. E
16. D
17. C
18. B
19. A
20. D
21. E

The Pilgrims Essay

1. C
2. D
3. D
4. D
5. C
6. E
7. C
8. B
9. E
10. B
11. A
12. D
13. C
14. B
15. B
16. C
17. B
18. B
19. D
20. E

Brain Wave Research Essay

1. C
2. C
3. D
4. B
5. A
6. C
7. D
8. C
9. E
10. B
11. A
12. B
13. B
14. A
15. E
16. A
17. A
18. C
19. B
20. E

Cancer Risk Essay

1. B
2. D
3. A
4. B
5. C
6. E
7. B
8. B
9. D
10. E
11. C
12. A
13. C
14. B
15. D
16. C